MySQL and MariaDB for DBAs: Intermediate Operations and Tuning Techniques

James Relington

DEDICATION

To those who seek knowledge, inspiration, and new perspectives—
may this book be a companion on your journey, a spark for curiosity,
and a reminder that every page turned is a step toward discovery.

AKNOWLEDGEMENTS

I would like to express my deepest gratitude to everyone who contributed to the creation of this book. To my colleagues and mentors, your insights and expertise have been invaluable. A special thank you to my family and friends for their unwavering support and encouragement throughout this journey.

Understanding the MySQL and MariaDB Architecture

MySQL and MariaDB are two of the most widely used relational database management systems (RDBMS), with a shared lineage and a common architecture. The architecture of both databases is designed to provide a reliable, scalable, and high-performance environment for managing large sets of data. While the two share many similarities, MariaDB was created as a fork of MySQL after concerns arose regarding the acquisition of MySQL by Oracle Corporation. Despite this divergence, the fundamental architecture of MySQL and MariaDB remains largely the same, with both utilizing similar core components and technologies. Understanding the internal workings of MySQL and MariaDB is crucial for database administrators (DBAs) who wish to optimize performance, ensure data consistency, and troubleshoot effectively.

At the heart of both MySQL and MariaDB is the client-server architecture. This architecture separates the database management system's processes into two major components: the server and the client. The server is responsible for managing the database, handling queries, and maintaining the integrity and consistency of the data. It runs as a background process on the machine, listening for incoming requests from clients. Clients, on the other hand, are applications or tools that interact with the database server, sending queries, retrieving results, and performing other database operations. The client-server model allows for communication over a network, making it possible for multiple clients to interact with a single database server, whether they are local or remote.

The MySQL and MariaDB server processes are organized into several layers that interact with one another to perform the various tasks associated with database operations. These layers include the SQL layer, the optimizer, the storage engine layer, and the I/O layer. Each layer has a specific responsibility, and together they work in tandem to ensure the efficiency and reliability of the database system.

The SQL layer is the topmost layer in the MySQL and MariaDB architecture. It is responsible for parsing and interpreting SQL queries submitted by the client. When a query is received, the SQL layer performs syntax checks to ensure the query is valid. If the query is correct, the SQL layer passes it on to the query optimizer. The SQL layer also manages user authentication and authorization, ensuring that only authorized users can access the database.

The query optimizer is one of the most important components of the database server. Its job is to determine the most efficient way to execute a query. It does this by analyzing the SQL query and considering various possible execution plans. The optimizer looks at factors such as the structure of the query, the available indexes, the size of the tables, and the distribution of data in the tables to determine the best execution strategy. The goal of the optimizer is to minimize the time and resources required to execute a query, improving overall performance.

Once the query optimizer has selected an execution plan, the query is passed to the storage engine layer. The storage engine is responsible for managing how data is stored and retrieved from disk. MySQL and MariaDB support a variety of storage engines, each with its own characteristics and performance characteristics. The most commonly used storage engine is InnoDB, which supports transactions, foreign keys, and row-level locking, making it a good choice for high-performance, transactional applications. Other storage engines, such as MyISAM and Aria, are available for specific use cases, such as non-transactional workloads or full-text search.

The storage engine is responsible for reading and writing data to disk, as well as handling the underlying data structures such as tables, indexes, and logs. It is also responsible for implementing transaction management, ensuring data consistency and durability. InnoDB, for example, uses a write-ahead logging (WAL) mechanism to ensure that changes to the database are logged before they are written to the data files, providing durability in case of a system crash.

Underneath the storage engine layer lies the I/O layer, which is responsible for managing the input and output operations between the server and the storage media. This layer interacts directly with the operating system's file system to read and write data from disk. The I/O layer is crucial for database performance, as disk I/O is often one of the most significant bottlenecks in database systems. Optimizing the I/O layer is therefore essential for improving overall database performance.

In addition to these core layers, MySQL and MariaDB also incorporate various other components that enhance their functionality and performance. For example, both systems include a query cache, which stores the results of previously executed queries in memory. When an identical query is received, the server can return the cached result rather than re-executing the query, significantly improving response times for frequently executed queries. MySQL and MariaDB also include support for replication, allowing data to be copied from one server to another for redundancy, load balancing, or scalability purposes.

Another important aspect of MySQL and MariaDB's architecture is their support for multi-threading. The server processes queries using multiple threads, allowing for parallel execution of multiple queries at the same time. This approach enhances the ability of the system to handle a high volume of concurrent connections and queries, making MySQL and MariaDB suitable for large-scale applications. The ability to manage multiple threads is also important for ensuring that the database server remains responsive under heavy loads, as it can distribute the workload across available CPU cores.

The architecture of MySQL and MariaDB also places a strong emphasis on data consistency and durability. Both systems use the ACID properties (Atomicity, Consistency, Isolation, Durability) to ensure that database transactions are processed reliably. InnoDB, the default storage engine for both MySQL and MariaDB, supports full ACID compliance, which guarantees that transactions are processed in a way that ensures data integrity, even in the event of system crashes or power failures.

For DBAs, understanding the architecture of MySQL and MariaDB is essential for optimizing the performance and reliability of the database. By understanding how queries are processed, how data is stored and retrieved, and how the different components interact, DBAs can make informed decisions about configuration, tuning, and troubleshooting. This knowledge allows them to address performance bottlenecks, improve query execution times, and ensure that the database system operates efficiently, even under heavy workloads. The flexibility and scalability of MySQL and MariaDB's architecture make them ideal choices for a wide range of applications, from small websites to large-scale enterprise systems.

Configuring MySQL and MariaDB for Optimal Performance

Configuring MySQL and MariaDB for optimal performance requires a deep understanding of the system's architecture, workload, and the specific hardware on which the databases run. Both MySQL and MariaDB offer a wide range of configuration options that can be adjusted to improve the efficiency of query processing, I/O operations, memory usage, and overall system responsiveness. By carefully tuning the parameters of the database server, DBAs can ensure that the system performs efficiently under various conditions, from low-traffic environments to high-demand applications. This process involves analyzing several factors, such as memory allocation, query cache, storage engines, and connection settings.

One of the first areas to consider when optimizing MySQL and MariaDB performance is memory management. Both systems allow administrators to adjust memory buffers to accommodate the database's needs. The InnoDB buffer pool is perhaps the most important memory-related setting, as it determines how much memory will be allocated to store cached data and indexes. A larger buffer pool allows the database to cache more data in memory, reducing the need for disk I/O and improving performance. However, allocating too much memory to the buffer pool can lead to resource contention, causing the operating system to swap memory to disk, which significantly slows down performance. Therefore, it is essential to find a balance that maximizes memory usage without over-committing system resources. The general recommendation is to allocate about 60-70% of available system memory to the InnoDB buffer pool, although this figure can vary based on workload and available resources.

Beyond the InnoDB buffer pool, MySQL and MariaDB provide several other memory-related settings that can affect performance. The query cache is another important feature, especially in read-heavy environments. The query cache stores the results of frequently executed queries in memory, allowing the server to return results instantly without having to re-execute the query. However, for write-intensive workloads, the query cache can become a bottleneck, as it needs to be invalidated each time data is modified. In such cases, disabling the query cache or fine-tuning its parameters can lead to better performance.

Another critical area for optimization is the storage engine configuration. Both MySQL and MariaDB support a variety of storage engines, with InnoDB being the default choice for most applications. InnoDB is a transactional storage engine that supports features such as ACID compliance, foreign key constraints, and row-level locking, making it suitable for high-performance, mission-critical applications. However, tuning InnoDB's parameters is essential to fully leverage its capabilities. The InnoDB log file size, for example, plays a crucial role in write performance. Larger log files can improve write throughput, but they also consume more disk space. Configuring the log file size properly helps strike a balance between write performance and disk space usage.

Another aspect of storage engine optimization involves the InnoDB flush method and flush log at trx commit settings. The flush method controls how data is written to disk, and the flush log at trx commit setting determines how often the transaction log is written to disk. These parameters should be adjusted based on the server's workload. For write-heavy environments, increasing the flush log at trx commit setting can reduce the number of disk writes, improving performance. However, this must be done with caution, as it may affect the durability of transactions in the event of a crash.

Disk I/O is often one of the most significant performance bottlenecks in database systems. To optimize I/O, both MySQL and MariaDB provide several options for configuring how data is read from and written to disk. Using the InnoDB file-per-table mode can improve I/O performance by storing each table's data in its own file, rather than sharing a single tablespace. This setup reduces contention for disk resources, particularly in environments with high read/write activity. Additionally, adjusting the innodb_io_capacity parameter allows administrators to limit the number of I/O operations performed by InnoDB, preventing disk overloading and ensuring more consistent performance.

Connection settings are another area that can greatly influence database performance. MySQL and MariaDB servers can handle a large number of concurrent connections, but managing this properly is crucial. Each connection requires memory and system resources, and a high number of connections can quickly overwhelm the server if it is not configured to handle them effectively. The max_connections setting controls the maximum number of concurrent connections the server will allow. Setting this parameter too high can lead to resource exhaustion, while setting it too low can cause clients to be denied access when the server is under heavy load. Adjusting the thread cache size and connection buffer sizes can also improve performance by reducing the overhead associated with establishing new connections.

Another key aspect of MySQL and MariaDB performance optimization is the query execution process. By adjusting the optimizer settings, DBAs can influence how queries are executed and ensure they are processed as efficiently as possible. The join_buffer_size, sort_buffer_size, and read_rnd_buffer_size settings are important for optimizing join and sorting operations. These buffers determine the amount of memory allocated for operations that involve scanning and sorting large datasets. Increasing these buffer sizes can improve the performance of complex queries, but allocating too much memory can result in excessive memory consumption. Monitoring the performance of individual queries using the EXPLAIN statement helps identify bottlenecks and can guide further optimization.

In addition to the configuration settings within MySQL and MariaDB, hardware considerations play a significant role in performance. Using solid-state drives (SSDs) rather than traditional hard drives can significantly speed up I/O operations. SSDs have much faster read and write speeds, which can reduce disk latency and improve overall database performance. Additionally, ensuring that the system has adequate CPU resources and sufficient RAM is essential for handling high query loads and large datasets. For systems with very large databases, adding additional CPU cores or increasing memory capacity can provide substantial performance improvements.

Replication and clustering are other aspects of MySQL and MariaDB that can benefit from optimization. In replication environments, configuring the server to use asynchronous or semi-synchronous replication can improve performance by reducing the impact of network latency. By tuning replication settings such as the binlog_format and sync_binlog parameters, DBAs can optimize the replication process for their specific workload, ensuring minimal lag between the master and slave servers.

Finally, regular maintenance tasks such as indexing, query optimization, and database housekeeping are crucial for long-term performance. Indexing ensures that frequently queried data can be retrieved quickly, while query optimization involves refining slow or inefficient queries to reduce their execution time. Routine database housekeeping, such as optimizing tables and removing unused data, helps prevent performance degradation over time.

Achieving optimal performance in MySQL and MariaDB requires ongoing attention to configuration settings, hardware resources, and workload characteristics. By fine-tuning the various parameters and considering the specific demands of the system, DBAs can maximize the efficiency of their databases, ensuring they perform well under varying conditions and workloads.

Advanced Indexing Techniques in MySQL and MariaDB

Indexing is a crucial aspect of optimizing database performance, especially in MySQL and MariaDB, where large datasets are often queried and manipulated. At its core, indexing enables the database engine to quickly locate and retrieve data without having to scan the entire table. While basic indexing techniques, such as primary and unique indexes, are essential, advanced indexing techniques provide even greater performance improvements. These techniques are particularly useful in complex queries involving large volumes of data or queries that need to be executed rapidly in real-time environments. Understanding the underlying principles of indexing and employing advanced strategies is key for DBAs who want to maximize database performance.

One of the most important advanced indexing techniques involves the use of composite indexes. A composite index, or multi-column index, allows the database to index multiple columns at once. This is particularly useful in queries that filter or sort data based on several columns. For example, if a query frequently filters data using a combination of the columns "first_name" and "last_name," creating a composite index on both columns will improve the query performance significantly. However, composite indexes should be carefully designed, as they are most effective when the columns involved are used together in query conditions. In cases where columns are not queried together often, the composite index may not provide the desired performance improvement. Additionally, the order of the columns in the composite index matters. MySQL and MariaDB use a left-to-right matching strategy when applying a composite index, so the order of the columns in the index should reflect the typical query patterns.

Another advanced indexing technique is the use of full-text indexes. Full-text indexing is designed for use with text-based data, particularly for searching large blocks of text or documents. MySQL and MariaDB support full-text indexing with the InnoDB and MyISAM storage engines. Full-text indexes enable the database to perform efficient searches based on natural language queries, such as finding documents containing certain words or phrases. When creating a full-text index, the database engine builds an inverted index, which maps words to their locations in the text. This allows for fast searching and retrieval of text-based data. Full-text indexes can be particularly beneficial in content management systems, forums, or applications that involve searching large amounts of text. However, full-text indexes require significant storage space and memory, and they can impact write performance due to the overhead of maintaining the index. It is important to consider these trade-offs when deciding whether to implement full-text indexing in a system.

Spatial indexes are another advanced indexing option available in MySQL and MariaDB. These indexes are designed for handling spatial data, such as geographical coordinates or geometrical shapes. Spatial indexes use a different indexing structure known as R-trees, which are well-suited for multidimensional data. In MySQL and MariaDB, spatial indexes are commonly used with the MyISAM and InnoDB storage engines, although support for spatial indexes in InnoDB has improved in recent versions. These indexes allow for fast querying of spatial data, such as finding points within a certain distance of a location or identifying shapes that intersect with others. Applications such as geographic information systems (GIS) and location-based services benefit from spatial indexing, as it enables efficient processing of spatial queries. When working with spatial data, it is essential to ensure that the data types and indexing methods align with the specific use case, as spatial indexing techniques can be quite specialized.

Another critical technique in advanced indexing involves the use of covering indexes. A covering index is an index that contains all the columns needed to satisfy a query, meaning that the database does not need to access the actual table data. When a query can be satisfied entirely by an index, the database engine can avoid performing a costly table lookup. This can dramatically improve performance, especially for read-heavy workloads. Covering indexes are particularly useful when a query only involves columns that are part of an index, making them ideal for read-only operations or when fetching data from frequently accessed tables. The challenge with covering indexes is determining which columns to include in the index, as including too many columns can increase index size and maintenance overhead. Additionally, covering indexes work best when the index can satisfy the query in its entirety. For complex queries that require accessing multiple tables or large datasets, covering indexes may not always be the most efficient solution.

Reverse indexes, although less commonly used, are another advanced indexing technique that can improve performance in specific situations. A reverse index works by storing the reversed version of a string or text value in the index. This can be particularly useful when performing searches on values that are typically queried in reverse order, such as IP addresses or certain types of codes. For instance, when searching for records that start with a specific suffix rather than a prefix, reverse indexes allow for faster searches by matching the query pattern more efficiently. This type of index is relatively rare and may not be appropriate for all systems, but it can be useful for specialized use cases where reverse searches are common.

The use of partial indexes is another technique that can help optimize performance for specific queries. A partial index allows the creation of an index on a subset of the data, based on a condition or filter. This is useful when a table contains large amounts of data but queries often focus on a specific subset of rows. For example, a partial index could be created to index only rows that meet certain criteria, such as records with a specific status or rows created within a certain date range. Partial indexes can significantly reduce the size of the index and improve query performance by excluding irrelevant rows from the index. However, partial indexes require careful planning to ensure they are used effectively and that the conditions applied to the index match the typical query patterns.

Index maintenance is also an essential consideration in advanced indexing techniques. As data in a table grows, indexes can become fragmented, leading to performance degradation. Regular index optimization is necessary to ensure that indexes remain efficient over time. This process involves rebuilding or defragmenting indexes to remove inefficiencies and improve lookup times. In MySQL and MariaDB, the OPTIMIZE TABLE command can be used to rebuild indexes and reclaim space. Additionally, monitoring index usage is important to identify underutilized or redundant indexes that can be removed to reduce overhead and improve overall system performance.

Ultimately, advanced indexing techniques in MySQL and MariaDB offer DBAs the tools to enhance query performance, reduce latency, and efficiently handle large datasets. By strategically implementing composite, full-text, spatial, and covering indexes, along with understanding specialized options like reverse and partial indexes, database administrators can create highly optimized environments that support the needs of complex applications. The key to successful indexing lies in understanding the query patterns, data types, and workload characteristics of the system. With careful planning and continual monitoring, advanced indexing can significantly improve the performance and scalability of MySQL and MariaDB databases.

Query Optimization: Techniques for Faster Execution

Query optimization is one of the most crucial aspects of database performance tuning. In MySQL and MariaDB, poorly optimized queries can lead to slow response times, increased resource consumption, and unnecessary load on the server. A slow query can have a cascading effect, especially in high-traffic environments where numerous queries are being executed concurrently. Optimizing queries ensures that they run more efficiently, requiring less CPU time, memory, and I/O resources. This process is vital for databases with large datasets or complex transactions, where query performance can directly impact the user experience and overall system efficiency.

The first step in optimizing a query is to understand how the database engine processes it. Both MySQL and MariaDB use a query execution plan to determine how a given SQL query will be executed. This plan is generated by the query optimizer, which analyzes the query's structure and considers various execution strategies to identify the most efficient path for retrieving the requested data. DBAs can inspect this execution plan using the EXPLAIN statement, which provides valuable information about how a query will be executed, including details on table scans, index usage, join types, and sorting. By analyzing the execution plan, DBAs can identify bottlenecks and areas for improvement, such as missing indexes, inefficient joins, or unnecessary full table scans.

One of the most effective techniques for optimizing queries is the use of indexes. Indexes allow the database to quickly locate data without scanning the entire table. For example, when a query involves searching for specific values in a column, an index can significantly speed up the search process by allowing the database to perform a direct lookup instead of performing a sequential scan. The key to optimizing queries with indexes is to create them strategically. Indexes should be created on columns that are frequently used in WHERE clauses, JOIN conditions, or ORDER BY clauses. However, it is essential to avoid over-indexing, as too many indexes can degrade performance, especially for write-heavy operations. Additionally, the order of columns in composite indexes should align with the query patterns, as MySQL and MariaDB optimize queries by scanning indexes from left to right.

Another critical technique in query optimization is reducing the number of rows processed. The more data a query needs to process, the longer it will take to execute. One way to achieve this is by using selective filtering in the WHERE clause. By specifying precise conditions, queries can reduce the amount of data they need to scan, which improves performance. Additionally, using LIMIT clauses can help restrict the number of rows returned by the query, which can be particularly useful when testing or retrieving only a subset of results. Optimizing the SELECT statement by selecting only the necessary columns is also important. Rather than using SELECT *, which returns all columns in a table, selecting only the required columns reduces the amount of data transferred from the database to the client, improving both speed and efficiency.

The structure of the query itself plays a significant role in its execution time. Complex queries involving multiple joins, subqueries, and aggregations can be particularly slow if they are not optimized properly. One way to optimize complex queries is to break them into smaller, simpler parts. Subqueries can sometimes be rewritten as joins, which are often more efficient. Similarly, queries that use GROUP BY or ORDER BY clauses can benefit from indexing the relevant columns to speed up the aggregation and sorting processes. When dealing with multiple joins, it is crucial to ensure that the tables are joined in the most efficient order. MySQL and MariaDB typically process joins from left to right, so joining smaller tables first can help reduce the overall execution time.

Another optimization strategy involves minimizing the use of subqueries, especially when they can be replaced with joins or temporary tables. While subqueries are often convenient and easy to write, they can be less efficient than alternative methods. For example, subqueries in the SELECT clause can cause the database to repeatedly scan the same data, leading to unnecessary overhead. By replacing subqueries with joins or by using derived tables, which are temporary result sets stored in memory, queries can often be optimized for faster execution. Additionally, using EXISTS or IN instead of a subquery in the WHERE clause can improve performance, as these operators are typically more efficient in terms of execution.

Query optimization also involves making use of the appropriate storage engine for the workload. While InnoDB is the default and most commonly used storage engine in MySQL and MariaDB, other storage engines like MyISAM or Aria may be more suitable for certain use cases, such as read-heavy workloads or when transaction support is not required. The choice of storage engine affects how indexes are handled, how data is stored and retrieved, and how locking and concurrency are managed. For instance, InnoDB uses row-level locking, which is beneficial in highly concurrent environments, while MyISAM uses table-level locking, which may be more efficient in scenarios with low concurrency but heavy read operations.

Optimizing the use of temporary tables is another critical factor in query performance. MySQL and MariaDB create temporary tables in memory when queries involve sorting or grouping large result sets. However, when these tables exceed a certain size, they are written to disk, which can cause significant performance degradation. To optimize query performance, it is essential to ensure that temporary tables are created efficiently and that their size does not exceed the available memory. Adjusting the tmp_table_size and max_heap_table_size variables can help prevent temporary tables from being written to disk by increasing the available memory for in-memory temporary tables. In cases where temporary tables are unavoidable, using the MEMORY storage engine for temporary tables can improve performance by keeping them entirely in memory.

Another important consideration is the use of query caching, which can significantly reduce the execution time of frequently executed queries. MySQL and MariaDB support query caching, where the results of a query are stored in memory, and subsequent identical queries are served from the cache rather than being re-executed. This can be particularly beneficial for read-heavy workloads where the same queries are executed repeatedly. However, query caching can introduce overhead in write-heavy environments, as the cache needs to be invalidated every time data is modified. Adjusting the query_cache_size and query_cache_type parameters allows DBAs to control the query cache's behavior and optimize its usage based on the workload.

Finally, keeping the database schema and data model well-organized is fundamental to query optimization. A well-designed schema reduces redundancy, minimizes the need for complex joins, and improves the ability to index relevant columns. Normalization is essential for ensuring that the data model is efficient and scalable, while denormalization may be useful in some cases to optimize read-heavy queries by reducing the need for complex joins. Properly maintaining the database by removing unused indexes, archiving old data, and updating statistics helps ensure that the database continues to perform well as it grows.

Query optimization is an ongoing process that requires monitoring and adjustments over time. By understanding how MySQL and MariaDB process queries, DBAs can use various techniques to improve query performance, reduce server load, and provide a better user experience. With careful analysis and tuning, even complex queries can be made to run much more efficiently.

Understanding the Query Execution Plan

The query execution plan is one of the most powerful tools available to database administrators and developers for optimizing query performance. In MySQL and MariaDB, a query execution plan reveals how the database engine interprets and executes a particular SQL query. By analyzing the execution plan, administrators can identify inefficiencies, such as unnecessary full table scans, improper use of indexes, or inefficient join operations. The query execution plan is a detailed roadmap that shows the steps the database will take to retrieve the requested data, allowing users to understand the inner workings of their queries and make informed decisions on how to improve performance.

When a SQL query is executed in MySQL or MariaDB, the database engine uses an internal query optimizer to determine the most efficient way to execute the query. The optimizer analyzes the query's structure, the available indexes, the distribution of data in the tables, and other factors to generate an execution plan. This plan is not static; rather, it can vary depending on the query, the size of the dataset, and the database schema. By default, MySQL and MariaDB use a cost-based optimizer, which attempts to minimize the total cost of executing the query, where cost is measured in terms of CPU time, I/O operations, and memory usage.

To understand the execution plan, users can use the EXPLAIN statement in MySQL or MariaDB. When placed before a query, EXPLAIN provides a detailed breakdown of how the database engine will execute the query. The output of EXPLAIN includes various columns that describe each step of the execution process. These columns include the table being accessed, the type of join being used, the number of rows being examined, the index being used (if any), and the estimated cost of the operation. Each of these elements provides valuable insights into how the database will retrieve the requested data and where potential performance bottlenecks may lie.

One of the most important pieces of information in the query execution plan is the join type. MySQL and MariaDB use different types of joins, each with varying levels of efficiency. The most efficient join is the "const" join, which occurs when the database can quickly find a single row based on a primary key or unique index. Other join types include "ref," "range," "index," and "all." A "ref" join indicates that the database has used an index to retrieve matching rows, while a "range" join is used when the query includes a range condition (e.g., greater than or less than). An "index" join means that the database is scanning an index to retrieve the necessary data, and an "all" join indicates a full table scan, which is the least efficient join type.

The execution plan also provides information about the number of rows being examined during the query execution process. This is crucial for understanding how much data the database is processing, which directly impacts query performance. The number of rows is estimated based on the statistics available to the optimizer, which are gathered from the table's data distribution. If the query involves filtering or sorting data, the database engine will use indexes to minimize the number of rows that need to be examined. However, if no suitable indexes exist or if the optimizer chooses a suboptimal execution path, the database may resort to scanning large portions of the table, which can lead to significant performance degradation.

Indexes play a critical role in the query execution plan. When a query includes a condition that matches a column indexed by the database, the execution plan will show that the index is being used to retrieve the relevant rows more efficiently. If an index is not being used, the execution plan will indicate that a full table scan is being performed. This could be due to several factors, such as the lack of an appropriate index, the database's decision to avoid using the index for performance reasons, or the query's inability to utilize the index effectively. In such cases, it may be necessary to create a new index or modify the query to ensure that the existing indexes are used effectively.

One of the most powerful features of the query execution plan is its ability to show whether the optimizer has chosen the most efficient index for the query. In some cases, MySQL or MariaDB may choose a non-optimal index, or it may fail to use an index at all. This can occur due to outdated or incomplete statistics, which may lead the optimizer to make suboptimal decisions. DBAs can address this issue by running the ANALYZE TABLE command to update the table's statistics, ensuring that the optimizer has accurate information when generating the execution plan. In some cases, forcing the optimizer to use a specific index using the FORCE INDEX directive in the query can also help improve performance.

Another critical aspect of the execution plan is the sorting and filtering of data. Queries that include ORDER BY, GROUP BY, or DISTINCT clauses may require additional steps to sort or group the data before returning the result set. In some cases, the database can perform these operations efficiently by utilizing indexes. However, if the query requires sorting a large amount of data that is not indexed, the database may need to perform a costly sort operation. The execution plan will indicate whether the database is performing a file sort or using an index to retrieve the data in the desired order. To optimize such queries, DBAs can create indexes on the columns used in the ORDER BY or GROUP BY clauses, allowing the database to retrieve the data in the correct order without needing to sort it afterward.

The query execution plan can also help identify the use of temporary tables. MySQL and MariaDB often create temporary tables when executing complex queries that involve sorting or grouping large result sets. Temporary tables are used to store intermediate results that are processed before returning the final result to the user. While temporary tables are useful for handling complex queries, they can also introduce overhead, particularly if the tables exceed the available memory and are written to disk. The execution plan will indicate whether temporary tables are being created and whether they are stored in memory or on disk. By optimizing the query to reduce the need for temporary tables or by increasing the available memory for in-memory temporary tables, DBAs can improve query performance.

The execution plan also provides valuable insights into the use of caching. MySQL and MariaDB cache the results of frequently executed queries to improve performance. If a query's execution plan indicates that a cached result is being used, this means that the database is retrieving the result from memory rather than re-executing the query. Query caching is particularly useful for read-heavy workloads, where the same queries are executed multiple times. However, query caching can introduce overhead in write-heavy environments, as the cache must be invalidated whenever data is modified. Understanding how the execution plan interacts with the query cache allows DBAs to fine-tune its behavior and maximize its effectiveness.

In summary, the query execution plan is a vital tool for understanding and optimizing query performance in MySQL and MariaDB. By carefully analyzing the execution plan, DBAs can identify inefficiencies, optimize index usage, minimize the number of rows processed, and ensure that the query is executed in the most efficient way possible. With this knowledge, database administrators can significantly improve the performance of their queries, leading to faster response times and a more efficient database environment.

Analyzing Slow Queries with EXPLAIN and Profiling

When managing a MySQL or MariaDB database, one of the most critical tasks for optimizing performance is identifying and resolving slow queries. Slow queries can severely impact the overall responsiveness of the database, especially in environments with high traffic or large datasets. Fortunately, both MySQL and MariaDB offer tools like EXPLAIN and profiling that can provide in-depth insights into how queries are executed, helping database administrators (DBAs) pinpoint inefficiencies and bottlenecks in the query execution process. By analyzing slow queries using these tools, DBAs can optimize queries and improve database performance.

The first tool for analyzing slow queries is the EXPLAIN statement. This powerful tool allows DBAs to examine the query execution plan, which shows how the database engine processes a specific SQL query. When executed before a query, EXPLAIN provides a detailed breakdown of the steps the database will take to retrieve the data. This information includes the type of join being used, the indexes being applied, and the estimated number of rows the query will examine. EXPLAIN is especially useful for identifying full table scans, which are one of the most common causes of slow query performance. A full table scan occurs when the database has to scan the entire table to find matching rows, rather than using an index, which is far more efficient.

The output of the EXPLAIN statement includes several columns, each of which provides valuable information about the query execution plan. For instance, the "id" column indicates the order in which the database will execute each part of a query, which is especially important for complex queries with multiple subqueries or joins. The "select_type" column shows the type of query being executed, such as a simple SELECT, a UNION, or a subquery. The "table" column lists the tables involved in the query, and the "type" column indicates the type of join used. The most efficient join types are "const" and "ref," while the least efficient is "ALL," which indicates a full table scan. Additionally, the "key" column shows the index being used for the query, and the "rows" column estimates how many rows will be scanned to satisfy the query.

By carefully analyzing these columns, DBAs can gain a deeper understanding of how a query is executed and where performance issues may lie. For example, if EXPLAIN shows that a query is performing a full table scan instead of using an index, the DBA can consider adding an appropriate index to speed up the query. Alternatively, if the query is performing multiple unnecessary joins or scanning too many rows, the DBA can rewrite the query to improve its efficiency. In many cases, EXPLAIN will reveal opportunities for optimization that would be difficult to identify through other means.

Another tool for analyzing slow queries is profiling, which provides more detailed performance metrics than EXPLAIN. Profiling in MySQL and MariaDB is a method of recording the time spent on each step of query execution, allowing DBAs to identify specific parts of the query that are taking longer than expected. Profiling is especially useful for understanding how much time is spent on each phase of the query, including parsing, optimizing, and executing the query. By capturing this information, DBAs can pinpoint areas where improvements can be made, such as reducing the time spent on sorting, joining, or scanning data.

To enable profiling, DBAs can execute the "SET PROFILING = 1;" command in MySQL or MariaDB, which will enable the profiling feature for the current session. Once profiling is enabled, the DBAs can run their queries as usual. Afterward, they can use the "SHOW PROFILE" command to view the profiling information for a specific query. This command displays a breakdown of the time spent on different stages of the query, including the time spent on parsing, compiling, and executing each part of the query. Profiling data can be valuable for understanding the specific operations that are consuming the most resources and for identifying areas that could benefit from optimization.

Profiling also allows DBAs to analyze multiple queries in a session, which can be particularly useful for diagnosing performance issues in complex applications with many queries being executed concurrently. By analyzing the profiling data for multiple queries, DBAs can identify patterns in query execution and determine whether certain types of queries are consistently slow. This information can guide decisions about optimizing specific queries or making broader changes to the database schema or indexing strategy.

While EXPLAIN and profiling are both incredibly powerful tools for query analysis, it is important to use them in conjunction with other performance monitoring techniques. For instance, MySQL and MariaDB offer slow query logs, which capture queries that take longer than a specified threshold to execute. These logs can be helpful for identifying queries that may not be immediately obvious through profiling or EXPLAIN, particularly if they are not executed frequently enough to appear in the profiling data. By enabling the slow query log and setting an appropriate threshold, DBAs can capture and analyze queries that may be causing performance issues over time.

In addition to the slow query log, MySQL and MariaDB also provide performance schema tables, which offer detailed information about server performance, including query execution. These tables can be queried to obtain real-time data on query performance, resource usage, and other server statistics. By combining the insights from the slow query log, EXPLAIN, profiling, and the performance schema, DBAs can gain a comprehensive view of the query performance and make data-driven decisions about how to optimize their database.

When analyzing slow queries, it is also important to consider the overall database design and indexing strategy. In many cases, slow queries are not just the result of inefficient SQL but are also influenced by how the data is structured and indexed. For example, a query that involves joining large tables without appropriate indexes may perform poorly, even if the SQL itself is well-written. In such cases, the solution may involve creating or modifying indexes to improve query performance. However, creating too many indexes can also have a negative impact on performance, particularly for write-heavy workloads, as the database has to maintain the indexes whenever data is modified.

Optimizing slow queries is an iterative process that often requires a combination of techniques. By using tools like EXPLAIN and profiling, DBAs can gain valuable insights into how queries are executed and where performance issues are occurring. With this information, they can make targeted improvements to queries, indexing strategies, and database design. As a result, query performance can be significantly enhanced, leading to faster response times, reduced resource consumption, and a more efficient database overall.

InnoDB Storage Engine: Tuning and Optimization

The InnoDB storage engine is the default storage engine for both MySQL and MariaDB, known for its support of ACID-compliant transactions, row-level locking, and foreign key constraints. It is designed for high performance and reliability, making it suitable for a wide range of applications, from small websites to large-scale enterprise systems. However, to achieve optimal performance, it is crucial to properly tune and optimize InnoDB settings. InnoDB's complex architecture requires a deep understanding of its configuration parameters, as improper tuning can lead to suboptimal performance and resource inefficiencies.

At the core of InnoDB's performance is the InnoDB buffer pool, which is responsible for caching data and indexes in memory. By default, InnoDB caches data and indexes in memory to avoid frequent disk I/O operations, which can be a significant performance bottleneck. The buffer pool is one of the most important parameters to tune for InnoDB, as it directly impacts the amount of data that can be stored in memory and the speed of data retrieval. The size of the buffer pool is typically set to a percentage of the available system memory. It is generally recommended to allocate 60-70% of the total system memory to the buffer pool, though this depends on the workload and available resources. If the buffer pool is too small, the database will frequently need to read data from disk, leading to slower performance. Conversely, allocating too much memory to the buffer pool can cause the operating system to swap memory to disk, which will negatively affect performance.

In addition to the buffer pool size, the buffer pool instances setting is also important for large, multi-core systems. The buffer pool can be split into multiple instances, allowing InnoDB to more efficiently utilize multiple CPU cores and handle concurrent read and write operations. By default, InnoDB uses a single buffer pool instance, but for systems with multiple CPU cores and large memory, increasing the number of buffer pool instances can improve performance. This setting helps distribute memory access across multiple threads, reducing contention and improving overall throughput.

Another critical aspect of InnoDB tuning is the InnoDB log file size. The log files store transactional data before it is written to the database, and they are essential for ensuring durability and crash recovery. By adjusting the log file size, DBAs can influence the performance of write-heavy workloads. If the log files are too small, InnoDB will need to flush logs to disk more frequently, which can lead to increased disk I/O and slower performance. On the other hand, setting the log file size too large can lead to longer recovery times in the event of a crash. A typical recommendation is to set the log file size to 256MB to 1GB, but this will depend on the workload and available disk space.

InnoDB's transaction log flushing behavior is also an important tuning parameter. The flush log at trx commit setting controls when the transaction logs are written to disk. The default setting, which is to flush the log on every transaction commit, ensures durability but can increase disk I/O. In environments where performance is a higher priority than strict durability, setting this parameter to 2 can help reduce the number of disk flushes, as it writes the log to disk less frequently. This tradeoff should be carefully considered based on the application's requirements for data integrity and durability.

Another important area to consider is the InnoDB I/O operations. InnoDB uses a write-ahead logging (WAL) mechanism, where changes are first written to the log files before being written to the data files. This helps ensure that data can be recovered after a crash. However, excessive I/O can negatively impact performance, especially on systems with slower disk subsystems. InnoDB's I/O operations can be optimized by adjusting the innodb_io_capacity setting, which controls the number of I/O operations that InnoDB performs per second. By default, this setting is relatively low, but it can be increased for systems with high-performance disk subsystems, such as solid-state drives (SSDs). Increasing this setting allows InnoDB to perform more I/O operations in parallel, improving performance on write-heavy workloads.

InnoDB also uses a flush method to control how data is written to disk. The flush method can be set to "fsync" or "O_DIRECT," with the latter being the preferred option for systems using SSDs. Using O_DIRECT bypasses the operating system's file system cache, which can improve performance by reducing double caching of data. On systems with traditional hard drives, the fsync method may be more appropriate, as it ensures that writes are synced to disk before returning control to the application. DBAs should test both methods to determine which one provides better performance for their particular environment.

Another critical area for InnoDB optimization is the use of indexes. Indexes are vital for query performance, but they come with overhead. While indexes speed up SELECT queries, they can slow down INSERT, UPDATE, and DELETE operations because the indexes need to be updated every time data is modified. InnoDB supports several types of indexes, including primary key indexes, unique indexes, and full-text indexes. The choice of index type and the columns selected for indexing can have a significant impact on query performance. To optimize performance, DBAs should carefully analyze the query patterns and ensure that the appropriate indexes are in place. It is important to balance the number of indexes to avoid excessive overhead on write operations while ensuring that the most frequently queried columns are indexed.

The use of foreign keys in InnoDB can also affect performance. Foreign key constraints ensure data integrity by enforcing relationships between tables, but they come with an overhead. When a foreign key constraint is defined, InnoDB must check the integrity of the data whenever an insert, update, or delete operation is performed on the referenced tables. While this overhead is necessary for maintaining data consistency, it can impact performance, particularly in write-heavy environments. If foreign key constraints are not necessary for the application, disabling them may improve performance.

Another important consideration is the management of deadlocks and locking. InnoDB uses row-level locking, which reduces contention and allows multiple transactions to modify different rows in the same table concurrently. However, deadlocks can still occur when two or more transactions hold locks on resources that each other's transactions need. InnoDB automatically detects deadlocks and rolls back one of the transactions to resolve the situation. To minimize deadlocks, DBAs can optimize the application to ensure that transactions acquire locks in a consistent order, reducing the likelihood of conflicts.

InnoDB also supports table compression, which can help reduce storage requirements for large tables. By enabling table compression, DBAs can reduce the disk space used by InnoDB tables, especially for read-heavy workloads. However, compression comes with a performance tradeoff, as it requires additional CPU resources to compress and decompress data. For systems where disk space is at a premium, enabling compression can be beneficial, but it is important to test the impact on performance to ensure it provides a net benefit.

InnoDB's tuning and optimization require a careful balancing act between memory usage, disk I/O, transaction durability, and indexing strategies. By adjusting the InnoDB buffer pool size, log file sizes, flush behavior, I/O settings, and index management, DBAs can significantly improve the performance of MySQL and MariaDB databases. However, it is essential to monitor the system regularly and adjust settings as the workload evolves, ensuring that the database continues to perform optimally as it grows. The flexibility and performance capabilities of InnoDB make it a powerful choice for modern database applications, and with the right optimizations, it can handle the most demanding workloads efficiently.

MyISAM Storage Engine: Performance Considerations

MyISAM is one of the oldest and most widely used storage engines in MySQL and MariaDB, particularly for applications that require fast read operations and do not rely heavily on transactions or foreign key constraints. Although InnoDB is the default storage engine in MySQL and MariaDB today, MyISAM remains a popular choice for applications where read performance is paramount, and the overhead of InnoDB's transactional capabilities is unnecessary. Understanding the performance considerations of MyISAM is crucial for DBAs who wish to optimize their database environments, as the engine has a unique set of characteristics that impact query execution, data integrity, and overall system performance.

One of the key advantages of MyISAM is its simplicity. Unlike InnoDB, MyISAM does not support transactions, which means that it has lower overhead for most operations. This simplicity allows MyISAM to provide faster read performance, especially for read-heavy workloads. In MyISAM, data is stored in a series of files: one for the table data, one for the indexes, and one for the table's metadata. This design makes it highly efficient for sequential read operations, as the data is stored in a relatively straightforward format without the added complexity of transactional logging or row-level locking.

The indexing system in MyISAM is another important factor influencing performance. MyISAM uses a non-clustered indexing method, which means that the indexes are stored separately from the data itself. While this can result in faster reads for certain types of queries, it can also increase the time needed to update or delete data. When a record is inserted, updated, or deleted in a MyISAM table, the index must also be modified, which can lead to higher overhead compared to engines like InnoDB, which manage indexes more efficiently with row-level locking. For applications that involve frequent updates or deletions, MyISAM may not be the best choice, as it can lead to locking contention and slower performance.

MyISAM also uses table-level locking, which can be a double-edged sword. On one hand, table-level locking is simple and efficient for operations that do not require high concurrency, such as read-heavy applications where data is not frequently modified. On the other hand, table-level locking can become a significant bottleneck when multiple clients are attempting to write to the same table simultaneously. In these situations, MyISAM's locking mechanism can severely limit performance and scalability, as only one thread can modify the table at a time. This makes MyISAM less suitable for write-heavy workloads or applications that require high levels of concurrency. In contrast, InnoDB uses row-level locking, which allows multiple transactions to modify different rows in the same table simultaneously, making it more efficient in high-concurrency environments.

The lack of transactional support in MyISAM also means that it does not provide features like rollback or crash recovery, which are crucial for ensuring data integrity in environments where transactions are used. When a crash occurs in a MyISAM table, the database may become inconsistent, and the data may need to be repaired. This is in contrast to InnoDB, which uses a write-ahead logging (WAL) mechanism to ensure that data is written to disk in a consistent and recoverable state. For applications that require strong data integrity and consistency, MyISAM may not be suitable unless specific precautions are taken to ensure that data is backed up and repaired regularly.

Despite its lack of transactional support, MyISAM does have some performance features that can improve efficiency, particularly in read-heavy environments. One such feature is the use of key caches. MyISAM uses a key cache to store index blocks in memory, reducing the need to access the disk for index lookups. By tuning the key buffer size, DBAs can improve performance for queries that rely heavily on indexed data. The key buffer should be set to a size that allows the most frequently accessed indexes to be stored in memory, reducing disk I/O. However, it is important to balance the size of the key buffer with the overall memory usage of the system, as setting it too high can lead to resource contention and memory swapping.

Another performance consideration for MyISAM is the storage format of the data files. MyISAM tables are typically stored in the .MYD (MyISAM Data) and .MYI (MyISAM Index) files. Over time, as data is modified, these files can become fragmented, leading to slower performance. This is particularly true for write-heavy applications, where data is frequently updated or deleted. To mitigate fragmentation, DBAs can use the OPTIMIZE TABLE command, which rebuilds the table and its indexes, reclaiming space and defragmenting the data files. Regularly optimizing tables can help maintain performance in MyISAM-based systems, particularly for tables that are subject to frequent updates.

The performance of MyISAM is also influenced by the disk I/O subsystem. Since MyISAM does not support transactions and uses table-level locking, it places less strain on the disk compared to engines like InnoDB. However, because MyISAM performs better with sequential reads and less frequent writes, it is important to ensure that the disk subsystem can handle the volume of read operations. Using solid-state drives (SSDs) can provide a significant boost in read performance, particularly for large datasets. Additionally, DBAs should monitor disk I/O closely and ensure that disk throughput is sufficient to support the read demands of MyISAM-based applications.

Another consideration is the use of MyISAM's full-text search capabilities. MyISAM supports full-text indexes, which are particularly useful for applications that need to search large volumes of text, such as content management systems or document storage systems. Full-text indexes allow MyISAM to quickly retrieve records that match specific keywords or phrases. However, full-text indexing can consume significant resources, particularly for large datasets. DBAs should carefully consider the tradeoff between indexing for fast search performance and the overhead required to maintain the full-text index. Proper tuning of the full-text index size and usage patterns can help optimize the performance of queries that rely on text searching.

In MyISAM, the maximum row size and table size can also impact performance, especially for large tables. MyISAM supports large tables, but when tables exceed certain sizes, performance can begin to degrade, particularly if queries are not optimized to handle the larger datasets. Partitioning tables can be an effective strategy for managing large datasets and improving query performance. By partitioning large MyISAM tables, DBAs can reduce the amount of data scanned by queries, as each partition can be queried independently.

In sum, while MyISAM is a fast and simple storage engine that excels in read-heavy environments with relatively low write and concurrency requirements, it does have several limitations that must be considered for performance optimization. By carefully tuning key parameters such as the key buffer size, monitoring disk I/O performance, optimizing tables to reduce fragmentation, and evaluating the use of full-text indexing, DBAs can achieve significant performance improvements in MyISAM-based systems. However, it is important to weigh these benefits against MyISAM's limitations in write-heavy, high-concurrency environments and consider alternatives such as InnoDB when higher levels of transactional support and concurrent access are needed.

Managing Memory Allocation for MySQL and MariaDB

Memory management is one of the most critical aspects of optimizing the performance of MySQL and MariaDB databases. Effective memory allocation allows these systems to handle large datasets efficiently, process queries quickly, and ensure smooth performance in production environments. Poor memory management, on the other hand, can lead to significant performance issues such as excessive swapping, slow query response times, and overall system instability. Since both MySQL and MariaDB rely heavily on memory to store data, indexes, query results, and connection-related information, understanding how memory is allocated and how it can be optimized is essential for database administrators (DBAs) looking to maximize their database performance.

At the heart of memory management in MySQL and MariaDB is the allocation of memory buffers. These buffers are used to store various types of data, including query cache, indexes, and result sets, to reduce the need for disk I/O operations. The most important memory allocation for MySQL and MariaDB is the InnoDB buffer pool. The InnoDB buffer pool stores data and index pages in memory, which allows faster access to frequently queried data. The larger the buffer pool, the more data can be cached, which reduces disk I/O and significantly improves query performance. By default, MySQL and MariaDB allocate a portion of the system memory to the InnoDB buffer pool, but DBAs should manually tune this allocation to match the size of their working dataset and the available system memory.

The general recommendation for setting the size of the InnoDB buffer pool is to allocate between 60% and 80% of the total available system memory, particularly on dedicated database servers. This range helps ensure that there is enough memory available for other processes, including the operating system and client connections. However, the optimal buffer pool size can vary depending on the specific workload. For systems with large datasets or heavy read operations, increasing the buffer pool size can result in significant performance improvements. Conversely, for systems with small datasets or limited memory, reducing the buffer pool size may be necessary to avoid memory exhaustion.

In addition to the InnoDB buffer pool, MySQL and MariaDB allocate memory to several other areas, including sorting, joining, and temporary tables. Memory buffers used for these operations are essential for managing query execution and improving response times for complex queries. For example, when a query requires sorting large result sets or performing complex joins, MySQL and MariaDB use memory buffers to store intermediate results before returning the final output. These buffers are controlled by parameters such as sort_buffer_size, join_buffer_size, and read_rnd_buffer_size. These settings define the amount of memory allocated for sorting, joining, and reading operations, respectively.

The sort_buffer_size parameter determines the amount of memory allocated for sorting operations. Sorting is a critical operation for queries that include ORDER BY clauses or GROUP BY clauses. If the size of the result set exceeds the sort_buffer_size, MySQL and MariaDB will use temporary files on disk to complete the sort, which can significantly slow down query performance. Increasing the sort_buffer_size can improve performance for sorting large result sets, but allocating too much memory to this buffer can lead to memory contention, particularly in systems with many concurrent connections. Similarly, the join_buffer_size controls the amount of memory allocated for join operations. When executing queries that involve multiple tables, MySQL and MariaDB use this buffer to store intermediate results during the join process. Larger join buffers can speed up queries with complex join conditions, but again, allocating too much memory can lead to resource exhaustion.

The read_rnd_buffer_size parameter, on the other hand, controls the memory allocated for random reads of tables. This buffer is used when MySQL or MariaDB needs to read rows from a table in a non-sequential manner. For queries that require scanning a large number of rows with non-sequential access patterns, such as those that involve indexes or conditions on non-primary key columns, increasing the read_rnd_buffer_size can improve performance. However, as with the other memory buffers, setting this parameter too high can lead to excessive memory usage and cause the system to swap data to disk.

Another important area of memory allocation in MySQL and MariaDB is the memory allocated for client connections. Each client connection consumes memory, which is used to store session variables, query results, and other data related to the connection. The memory allocated for each connection is determined by the key_buffer_size (for MyISAM tables), thread_stack, and max_connections parameters. The key_buffer_size controls the amount of memory allocated for caching MyISAM index blocks, while the thread_stack controls the amount of memory allocated for each client thread's stack. The max_connections setting determines the maximum number of concurrent client connections the server will allow. If this value is set too high, it can lead to excessive memory usage, particularly when the number of active connections exceeds the system's available memory.

For systems with a large number of concurrent connections, managing memory usage becomes especially important. One way to manage memory for high-traffic applications is to adjust the thread_cache_size parameter. This parameter controls how many threads MySQL or MariaDB should cache for reuse. When a client connects to the server, a new thread is created to handle the connection. If thread_cache_size is set to a higher value, MySQL and MariaDB will reuse existing threads for new connections, reducing the overhead of creating and destroying threads. This can help reduce memory consumption and improve performance, especially on busy systems with frequent connections and disconnections.

Temporary tables also play a significant role in memory allocation in MySQL and MariaDB. When executing complex queries that involve sorting or grouping, MySQL and MariaDB may create temporary tables to store intermediate results. By default, temporary tables are created in memory, but if the result set is too large, the database engine will write the temporary table to disk. The size of in-memory temporary tables is determined by the tmp_table_size and max_heap_table_size parameters. If a temporary table exceeds these sizes, MySQL or MariaDB will write it to disk, which can cause performance degradation due to slower disk I/O. Increasing the tmp_table_size and max_heap_table_size parameters can help avoid this issue by allowing larger temporary tables to be created in memory.

In addition to these memory parameters, MySQL and MariaDB provide various other options for managing memory allocation for specialized operations. For example, the query_cache_size parameter controls the size of the query cache, which stores the results of SELECT queries to improve performance for repeated queries. The memory allocated to the query cache can be particularly beneficial in read-heavy applications where the same queries are executed frequently. However, for write-heavy workloads or applications that require frequent updates, the query cache may introduce overhead, as it needs to be invalidated whenever data changes. For such workloads, it may be best to disable the query cache altogether by setting query_cache_type to o.

Effective memory management for MySQL and MariaDB requires a careful balance between allocating sufficient memory for query processing, connection handling, and other database operations while avoiding memory exhaustion and excessive swapping. By understanding the various memory allocation parameters and their impact on performance, DBAs can fine-tune their databases to achieve optimal performance for their specific workloads. Regular monitoring and adjusting of memory settings based on system usage and traffic patterns can help maintain a stable and high-performance database environment.

Optimizing Disk I/O for Better Database Performance

Disk I/O is one of the most critical factors influencing the performance of MySQL and MariaDB databases. While in-memory operations such as caching and buffer pools significantly improve query performance, disk I/O still remains an inevitable part of database operations, especially when dealing with large datasets or when the available memory is exhausted. Efficient disk I/O management ensures that data can be read from and written to storage as quickly as possible, reducing query response times and ensuring smooth database operations. Proper optimization of disk I/O can make the difference between a sluggish, resource-heavy database and a high-performance system that handles large volumes of data efficiently.

One of the first steps in optimizing disk I/O is to assess the underlying hardware. The type of storage used has a significant impact on I/O performance. Traditional spinning hard drives (HDDs) have much slower read and write speeds compared to solid-state drives (SSDs). While HDDs may suffice for small databases or applications with minimal I/O requirements, SSDs provide much faster data access, resulting in quicker query responses and reduced latency. For databases that handle heavy read and write operations, upgrading to SSDs can provide a substantial boost in performance. SSDs have lower latency, faster random read and write speeds, and higher throughput, making them an excellent choice for I/O-intensive workloads. As database size grows and queries become more complex, the benefits of SSDs become increasingly apparent, particularly for read-heavy environments.

Another essential consideration for optimizing disk I/O is how data is stored and accessed by the database engine. MySQL and MariaDB use various storage engines, each with its own method of managing data. InnoDB, the default storage engine, uses a buffer pool to cache data in memory, reducing the need to perform disk reads. However, InnoDB still requires disk access for writing data and when the buffer pool cannot accommodate all the necessary data. MyISAM, another commonly used storage engine, stores data in separate files for the table and its index, which can affect I/O performance depending on how the data is accessed. In general, choosing the appropriate storage engine based on the workload is essential. InnoDB is typically the preferred option for transactional applications because of its support for ACID compliance and row-level locking, while MyISAM may be suitable for applications that prioritize fast read operations and do not require transaction support.

Optimizing disk I/O also involves understanding how MySQL and MariaDB handle disk writes. For instance, InnoDB uses a write-ahead logging (WAL) mechanism, which ensures that changes are first written to the transaction log before they are applied to the actual data files. This process helps ensure data durability and crash recovery but can also introduce overhead due to frequent disk writes. The size of the InnoDB log files and the frequency with which they are flushed to disk plays a significant role in performance. By adjusting the innodb_log_file_size parameter, DBAs can control the size of the log files. Larger log files can improve write performance by reducing the frequency of log flushes, but they also consume more disk space and increase recovery times in case of a crash. It is crucial to strike a balance that suits the workload requirements while minimizing disk I/O overhead.

The innodb_flush_log_at_trx_commit setting is another important parameter that affects disk I/O. This setting controls when the InnoDB transaction logs are flushed to disk. The default value of 1 ensures that the logs are flushed to disk after every transaction commit, which provides the highest level of data durability but may introduce additional disk I/O overhead. In write-heavy environments where performance is a higher priority than durability, setting this value to 2 or even 0 can reduce the frequency of disk writes, improving performance. However, these settings come with trade-offs in terms of data safety, as they may result in data loss in the event of a system crash.

In addition to tuning storage engines and transaction log settings, MySQL and MariaDB allow for the optimization of temporary tables, which are frequently used during complex queries that involve sorting or grouping. When a query requires sorting or joining large result sets, MySQL and MariaDB may create temporary tables to hold the intermediate results. By default, these temporary tables are stored in memory, but if the result set exceeds a certain size, the database engine will write the temporary tables to disk. Writing temporary tables to disk can significantly slow down query performance due to slower disk I/O. The tmp_table_size and max_heap_table_size parameters control the size of in-memory temporary tables, and increasing these values can help avoid disk writes for larger queries. However, increasing these parameters requires sufficient system memory to ensure that the database engine does not run out of available memory and cause system swapping.

Another method for optimizing disk I/O is through the use of partitioning. Partitioning involves dividing large tables into smaller, more manageable pieces, which can be stored on different disks or even on different servers. By partitioning large tables based on certain criteria (such as date ranges or key values), MySQL and MariaDB can limit the number of rows that need to be scanned for certain queries, reducing disk I/O and improving performance. For example, if a query only needs to access data within a specific range of dates, partitioning the table by date allows the database engine to scan only the relevant partitions, rather than the entire table. Partitioning can also improve parallelism in query execution, as different partitions can be processed simultaneously.

The use of indexing is another essential technique for reducing disk I/O. Indexes allow the database to quickly locate and retrieve data without having to scan the entire table. When a query includes conditions on indexed columns, MySQL and MariaDB can use the index to find matching rows more efficiently, reducing the amount of data that needs to be read from disk. However, indexes come with their own trade-offs. While they speed up read operations, they can slow down write operations, as the indexes need to be updated whenever data is modified. Therefore, it is essential to carefully choose which columns to index based on query patterns. Over-indexing can lead to unnecessary disk I/O overhead, particularly for write-heavy applications. A careful balance of indexing strategies based on the workload can significantly improve disk I/O performance.

Another important factor to consider is the use of RAID configurations for disk storage. RAID (Redundant Array of Independent Disks) is a data storage virtualization technology that combines multiple physical disks into a single logical unit for improved performance, redundancy, or both. RAID levels such as RAID 0, RAID 10, and RAID 5 offer various trade-offs between performance and data redundancy. For high-performance applications that require fast disk reads and writes, RAID 10 (a combination of mirroring and striping) is often recommended. RAID 10 offers both improved read and write performance and redundancy in case of disk failure, making it a suitable option for MySQL and MariaDB databases that handle large datasets and require high availability.

Finally, monitoring disk I/O performance is an ongoing task that requires regular attention. Tools such as the iostat command, the MySQL Performance Schema, and monitoring software can help DBAs track disk activity, identify bottlenecks, and optimize configurations. By regularly reviewing disk I/O performance metrics, DBAs can adjust parameters, optimize queries, and ensure that the database continues to perform optimally as the system grows.

Optimizing disk I/O is a multifaceted process that requires careful planning, configuration, and monitoring. By improving disk I/O, choosing the right hardware, optimizing storage engines, using efficient indexing strategies, and tuning various database parameters, DBAs can significantly improve MySQL and MariaDB performance. As database systems grow in size and complexity, ensuring that disk I/O is optimized becomes more critical for maintaining high performance and scalability.

Database Caching Strategies for MySQL and MariaDB

Caching is one of the most effective techniques for improving the performance of MySQL and MariaDB databases. It involves storing frequently accessed data in memory so that subsequent requests for the same data can be served much more quickly, reducing the need to perform expensive disk I/O operations. Caching is especially crucial for read-heavy applications, where the same data is accessed repeatedly, as it can drastically reduce query response times and decrease the overall load on the database server. Understanding how to implement and optimize caching strategies is essential for database administrators (DBAs) seeking to maximize the efficiency of their MySQL and MariaDB environments.

MySQL and MariaDB provide several caching mechanisms, each suited to different types of workloads and queries. One of the most widely used caching features is the query cache, which stores the results of SELECT queries in memory. When an identical query is issued again, the database can return the cached result without re-executing the query, which speeds up response times significantly. The query cache is particularly useful for read-heavy workloads where the same queries are executed multiple times. However, it is important to note that the query cache is not effective for write-heavy workloads, as any changes to the database, such as INSERT, UPDATE, or DELETE operations, invalidate the cache, forcing the query to be re-executed. Additionally, in MySQL and MariaDB versions starting from 5.7.20 and above, the query cache has been deprecated, and its use is not recommended for most modern applications. Disabling the query cache in such versions is often the best approach, as it may introduce unnecessary overhead.

Another critical caching strategy in MySQL and MariaDB is the InnoDB buffer pool. The buffer pool is used by the InnoDB storage engine to cache data and indexes in memory, reducing the need for disk I/O. Since the buffer pool can store frequently accessed data, it significantly improves the performance of SELECT queries by allowing them to retrieve data directly from memory rather than reading from disk. The size of the InnoDB buffer pool is one of the most important parameters to tune for MySQL and MariaDB performance. A larger buffer pool means that more data can be cached in memory, leading to faster query performance, especially for large databases. Typically, it is recommended to allocate between 60% and 70% of the system's total memory to the buffer pool on dedicated database servers, but this should be adjusted based on the size of the dataset and available resources. For systems with large working sets or memory-intensive workloads, increasing the buffer pool size can provide a noticeable improvement in performance.

In addition to the buffer pool, there are other memory buffers in MySQL and MariaDB that can be optimized for better caching. For example, the key cache in MyISAM is responsible for caching index blocks in memory, while the innodb_buffer_pool_size parameter controls the buffer pool size for the InnoDB storage engine. The innodb_sort_buffer_size and innodb_read_io_threads parameters also help manage caching during sorting and read operations. Properly configuring these buffers is crucial for efficient caching, as they help optimize data retrieval processes by keeping relevant data in memory. For databases with a high rate of insertions and updates, these buffers help maintain the necessary cache to support query performance without causing excessive disk I/O.

For applications that rely on complex queries, especially those involving large joins or aggregations, query results can also be cached at the application level. Many modern web applications use caching layers such as Memcached or Redis to store frequently queried data in memory. These caching systems are designed to provide ultra-fast access to data and can significantly reduce the number of database queries required for common operations. By caching the results of frequently executed queries at the application level, the database can handle fewer requests, freeing up resources for other operations and improving overall system performance. The data in these external caches can be synchronized with the database at regular intervals or on-demand, depending on the application's consistency requirements.

One of the most effective strategies for optimizing caching in MySQL and MariaDB is understanding and utilizing table and index caches. When working with large tables or complex data models, carefully crafted indexes can significantly speed up data retrieval. Indexing is an essential technique for improving query performance, but it can also impact caching efficiency. A well-designed index can help MySQL and MariaDB retrieve data faster, reducing the amount of time spent accessing disk storage. Indexes that align with the query patterns can help avoid full table scans and minimize disk I/O. In environments with a large number of concurrent queries, indexes on the most frequently queried columns can help maintain fast access speeds.

In addition to indexing, table partitioning is another strategy that can improve caching. Partitioning involves splitting a large table into smaller, more manageable pieces based on certain criteria, such as date ranges or key values. By partitioning tables, MySQL and MariaDB can optimize cache usage by reducing the amount of data that needs to be scanned for specific queries. For example, if a query only needs to access data from a certain range of dates, partitioning the table by date allows the database to scan only the relevant partition, which reduces the need for expensive disk I/O and improves caching efficiency. Partitioning can also help reduce memory pressure by allowing for parallel query execution across different partitions, making it easier to cache individual partitions rather than the entire table.

Disk I/O optimization also plays a crucial role in improving the effectiveness of caching strategies. While caching data in memory helps reduce disk access, some degree of disk I/O is inevitable, particularly for write-heavy operations or large datasets. Optimizing disk performance through the use of faster storage devices, such as solid-state drives (SSDs), can significantly enhance the performance of cached data. SSDs offer lower latency and faster read and write speeds compared to traditional hard disk drives (HDDs), which can further reduce the time required for data retrieval and ensure that the cache remains effective even under high workload conditions. Disk optimization, in conjunction with efficient memory caching strategies, can help maintain a balance between memory usage and storage access, resulting in faster response times and improved overall system performance.

Another caching strategy that should be considered is the use of materialized views. Materialized views store the results of a query as a static table, which can be periodically refreshed with new data. This strategy is beneficial for complex queries that involve joins, aggregations, or calculations, as it allows these results to be cached in the form of a table, reducing the need to recompute them on every request. While this approach may introduce some maintenance overhead due to the need to refresh the materialized view periodically, it can greatly improve performance for queries that are expensive to compute and are frequently executed.

Managing caching strategies in MySQL and MariaDB requires a deep understanding of the database's memory allocation and disk I/O behavior. Properly configuring the query cache, buffer pool, key cache, and external caching layers, as well as optimizing indexing and partitioning strategies, can lead to significant improvements in performance. At the same time, the choice of storage devices, memory allocation, and query execution plans all impact the effectiveness of caching. By carefully balancing these elements, DBAs can ensure that their databases perform at peak efficiency and handle high traffic loads with minimal latency. Effective caching strategies are key to ensuring that MySQL and MariaDB systems remain responsive and scalable, particularly in environments that deal with large datasets and complex queries.

Optimizing Table Scans and Index Usage

Optimizing table scans and index usage is critical for improving the performance of MySQL and MariaDB databases. As databases grow in size and complexity, queries that involve scanning large tables can become a significant bottleneck, leading to slower query response times and higher resource consumption. By using indexes effectively, reducing unnecessary table scans, and optimizing queries, database administrators (DBAs) can significantly enhance database performance, ensuring that queries execute quickly even in high-traffic environments.

When a query is executed in MySQL or MariaDB, the database engine must determine how to retrieve the requested data. If an index is available for the query's filtering conditions, the database can use the index to quickly locate the relevant data, avoiding the need for a full table scan. However, if no suitable index exists or if the query does not take advantage of available indexes, the database may resort to scanning the entire table, which can be highly inefficient, especially for large tables. This is where optimization strategies for table scans and index usage come into play. By carefully designing and maintaining indexes, as well as writing efficient queries, DBAs can minimize table scans and reduce the amount of data that needs to be processed.

One of the most effective ways to optimize table scans is through proper indexing. Indexes are used by the database to speed up data retrieval operations by providing a structured way to quickly locate rows that match a query's conditions. The choice of which columns to index is crucial for optimizing table scans. Indexes should be created on columns that are frequently used in WHERE clauses, JOIN conditions, or ORDER BY clauses. When a query includes conditions on indexed columns, the database can use the index to find matching rows more efficiently, significantly reducing the amount of data that needs to be scanned. For example, if a query frequently filters data by a customer's ID, creating an index on the customer_id column will allow the database to quickly locate the relevant rows without performing a full scan of the entire table.

In addition to indexing, the order of columns in composite indexes (indexes on multiple columns) also plays a critical role in query optimization. MySQL and MariaDB use a left-to-right matching strategy when applying composite indexes. This means that the order of the columns in the index should align with the query patterns. For instance, if a query filters data by both the customer_id and the order_date columns, creating a composite index on customer_id first and then order_date will allow the database to use the index efficiently. However, if the query filters by order_date first and then customer_id, the index may not be used effectively unless the columns in the composite index are reordered. Therefore, it is important to analyze query patterns carefully and design composite indexes that will be used effectively by the database engine.

Another key factor in optimizing table scans and index usage is understanding how MySQL and MariaDB decide whether to use an index or perform a table scan. The database engine uses a query optimizer to evaluate different execution plans and choose the most efficient one. The optimizer will decide to use an index if it determines that the index can significantly reduce the amount of data that needs to be scanned. However, in some cases, the optimizer may decide that a full table scan is more efficient, especially if the table is small or if the index is not selective enough. For example, if a query includes a condition on a column with a low cardinality (i.e., a column with very few unique values), the optimizer may choose a full table scan instead of using an index. In such cases, DBAs can improve performance by creating more selective indexes or adjusting the query to make better use of existing indexes.

The EXPLAIN statement is a valuable tool for analyzing query execution plans and understanding how MySQL and MariaDB are using indexes. When prefixed to a query, EXPLAIN provides detailed information about how the database will execute the query, including which indexes will be used, the type of join performed, and the estimated number of rows that will be scanned. By examining the EXPLAIN output, DBAs can identify potential performance bottlenecks, such as full table scans or inefficient index usage, and take steps to address them. For example, if EXPLAIN shows that the database is performing a full table scan instead of using an index, the DBA can consider creating a new index or modifying the query to make better use of the available indexes.

It is also important to avoid over-indexing, as creating too many indexes can lead to performance degradation, particularly for write-heavy workloads. Every time a row is inserted, updated, or deleted in a table, all associated indexes must be updated, which can introduce overhead. This overhead can slow down write operations, especially if the table has many indexes. Therefore, it is essential to carefully evaluate which columns need to be indexed based on the query patterns. Indexes should be created selectively, focusing on the columns that are most frequently used in query filtering, joining, and sorting.

In addition to creating the right indexes, optimizing the use of indexes also involves ensuring that the database engine can effectively use the available indexes. For example, queries that involve ranges (e.g., greater than or less than conditions) can benefit from range scans on indexed columns. If a query includes conditions on multiple columns, the database engine will evaluate which indexes to use based on the selectivity of the columns and the order in which they appear in the query. If the query includes functions or expressions that cannot take advantage of indexes, DBAs can consider rewriting the query to remove those functions or use indexed columns in the WHERE clause instead.

Another aspect of optimizing table scans and index usage is minimizing the number of joins and the complexity of the queries. Joins can often lead to large intermediate result sets that need to be scanned and processed, which can slow down performance. By reducing the number of joins or optimizing the join conditions, DBAs can improve query efficiency. For instance, using inner joins instead of outer joins can help reduce the number of rows processed, as outer joins involve additional data retrieval. Additionally, ensuring that join conditions use indexed columns can help reduce the amount of data that needs to be scanned for each join, improving overall query performance.

The use of partitioning can also help optimize table scans. Partitioning involves splitting large tables into smaller, more manageable pieces based on a specified key, such as a date or customer ID. This allows queries to scan only relevant partitions, rather than the entire table, which can reduce the amount of data that needs to be processed. For example, if a query filters data by date, partitioning the table by date allows the database to scan only the relevant partitions for the query, improving performance. Partitioning can be particularly useful for large tables that are frequently queried based on specific criteria, such as time periods or geographic regions.

Finally, regularly monitoring query performance and optimizing indexing strategies is essential for maintaining optimal database performance over time. As the dataset grows and query patterns change, indexes that were once effective may become less efficient. By periodically reviewing query performance and index usage, DBAs can ensure that the database continues to perform well and can make adjustments as needed to optimize table scans and index usage.

Optimizing table scans and index usage is a continuous process that requires careful planning, monitoring, and tuning. By selecting the right columns to index, analyzing query execution plans, and fine-tuning indexes and query structure, DBAs can significantly reduce table scans and improve query performance. Regular monitoring and adjustments based on workload changes are essential to ensuring long-term database efficiency.

Partitioning and Sharding in MySQL and MariaDB

Partitioning and sharding are advanced techniques used to enhance the scalability and performance of MySQL and MariaDB databases. As databases grow larger, traditional methods of managing data, such as storing everything in a single table or using a single server, can lead to performance bottlenecks. Partitioning and sharding address these issues by dividing large datasets into smaller, more manageable pieces, allowing for faster query execution, easier data management, and more efficient resource utilization. While both techniques share the goal of improving performance and scalability, they differ in how they manage data across multiple tables or servers.

Partitioning is the process of splitting a large table into smaller, more manageable parts called partitions. Each partition stores a subset of the data, and these partitions can be stored in different locations or even on different storage devices. Partitioning helps improve performance by reducing the amount of data that needs to be scanned for specific queries. When a query filters data based on certain criteria, MySQL or MariaDB can access only the relevant partitions, rather than scanning the entire table. This can significantly reduce query execution time, especially for large datasets or tables with millions of rows. Partitioning can also make maintenance operations, such as backups and data archiving, more efficient, as DBAs can work with individual partitions rather than the entire table.

There are several types of partitioning available in MySQL and MariaDB, including range partitioning, list partitioning, hash partitioning, and key partitioning. Range partitioning divides data into partitions based on a range of values, such as dates or numeric ranges. For example, a table storing sales data could be partitioned by month or year, allowing for faster querying of data from specific time periods. List partitioning is similar to range partitioning, but instead of using a continuous range, it divides the data into partitions based on a list of values, such as product categories or geographic regions. Hash partitioning evenly distributes data across partitions based on a hash function, ensuring that each partition has approximately the same amount of data. Key partitioning is similar to hash partitioning but uses MySQL's internal key function to determine how the data is distributed.

Each type of partitioning has its own advantages and is suited to different types of data and queries. For example, range partitioning is ideal for time-series data, where queries often filter by date. On the other hand, hash partitioning is better suited for evenly distributed datasets, where queries do not rely on specific ranges or values. Choosing the right partitioning strategy depends on the nature of the data, the query patterns, and the specific performance goals of the database.

While partitioning is a powerful tool for improving query performance within a single server, it does not address scalability issues when the database grows beyond the capabilities of a single machine. This is where sharding comes into play. Sharding is the process of distributing data across multiple servers, each of which stores a subset of the data. This technique helps scale out the database, enabling it to handle larger datasets and higher traffic loads by spreading the workload across multiple machines. Each server in a sharded setup is called a shard, and the data is distributed among the shards based on a sharding key.

The sharding key is a column or set of columns that determine how the data is distributed across the shards. For example, in an e-commerce application, the sharding key could be the customer_id, with each shard storing the data for a specific range of customer IDs. The key choice for sharding is critical, as it directly affects how evenly the data is distributed across the shards. If the sharding key results in an uneven distribution of data, some shards may become overloaded, leading to performance issues. Properly selecting the sharding key is essential for ensuring that the database scales effectively and that the workload is balanced across all shards.

Sharding offers several advantages, including the ability to scale horizontally by adding more servers as the database grows. This makes it an ideal solution for applications that need to handle large volumes of data or traffic that cannot be supported by a single server. Sharding also improves fault tolerance, as each shard is independent, and failure in one shard does not affect the others. However, sharding also introduces complexity in terms of data management and query execution. In a sharded setup, queries that need to access data from multiple shards must be carefully managed to ensure that they are executed efficiently. Additionally, sharding introduces challenges in terms of maintaining data consistency, as transactions that span multiple shards can be more complex to handle.

One of the key challenges of sharding is performing joins across multiple shards. Since each shard is a separate database instance, performing a join that involves data from two or more shards requires the database to query each shard individually, which can result in slower performance. To address this, sharded systems often rely on techniques such as denormalization, where data that is frequently joined is stored together on the same shard. This reduces the need for cross-shard joins, improving query performance. However, denormalization comes with trade-offs, as it can lead to data duplication and increased storage requirements.

Another challenge of sharding is managing transactions that span multiple shards. In a traditional database setup, transactions are typically handled by a single database instance, which ensures that all changes are committed or rolled back atomically. In a sharded setup, however, transactions that involve multiple shards require coordination between the shards, which can introduce overhead and increase complexity. To handle this, many sharded systems implement a two-phase commit protocol or similar mechanisms to ensure that transactions are properly coordinated and that data consistency is maintained across shards.

To manage sharding in MySQL and MariaDB, several third-party tools and frameworks are available. For example, ProxySQL is a popular tool that acts as a proxy between the application and the MySQL or MariaDB servers. It can be used to route queries to the appropriate shard based on the sharding key, ensuring that queries are executed on the correct server. Other tools, such as Vitess and MySQL Cluster, provide more advanced sharding and clustering capabilities, including automated shard management and load balancing.

While partitioning and sharding can significantly improve the performance and scalability of MySQL and MariaDB, they come with a set of challenges that must be carefully managed. Choosing the right partitioning and sharding strategies requires a deep understanding of the data, the queries, and the overall architecture of the application. Both techniques can be complex to implement and maintain, but when used correctly, they can provide substantial benefits in terms of scalability, performance, and fault tolerance. Whether partitioning a single large table or distributing data across multiple servers, both partitioning and sharding play a crucial role in enabling MySQL and MariaDB to scale effectively and handle large volumes of data and traffic.

Optimizing Join Performance in Complex Queries

Joins are fundamental in relational databases, enabling the combination of data from multiple tables based on certain conditions. In MySQL and MariaDB, joins are often used to retrieve related data spread across different tables, which is common in normalized database schemas. However, while joins are powerful and essential, they can become a performance bottleneck in complex queries, particularly when dealing with large datasets, multiple tables, and intricate join conditions. Optimizing join performance is crucial to ensuring that queries run efficiently and do not negatively impact overall system performance. By understanding the underlying mechanics of joins and applying effective optimization techniques, DBAs can significantly improve the speed of complex queries.

The first step in optimizing join performance is to understand the different types of joins used in MySQL and MariaDB. The most commonly used join types are INNER JOIN, LEFT JOIN, RIGHT JOIN, and CROSS JOIN. Each type has its own behavior and performance characteristics. INNER JOIN, for example, is typically the most efficient because it returns only rows where there is a match in both tables. However, even with INNER JOINs, the performance can degrade if the query involves multiple large tables or complex conditions. LEFT and RIGHT JOINs, on the other hand, return all rows from one table and the matching rows from the other table, leading to more data being processed and potentially slower performance. CROSS JOINs, which combine every row of one table with every row of another table, can cause significant performance issues due to the sheer volume of data they generate, especially when working with large tables.

One of the most important factors in optimizing join performance is ensuring that the relevant columns are indexed. Indexes help speed up data retrieval by allowing the database to quickly locate the rows that match the join condition, without having to scan the entire table. For instance, if a query joins two tables on the column "customer_id," creating an index on "customer_id" in both tables will significantly speed up the join operation. When a table has indexes on the join columns, MySQL or MariaDB can use these indexes to perform a much faster lookup instead of scanning all rows. However, indexing alone is not enough. The structure and order of the joins are also critical to how efficiently the query is executed.

The order in which tables are joined can have a significant impact on query performance. MySQL and MariaDB's query optimizer determine the join order, but in some cases, manual optimization can help improve efficiency. The database engine typically processes joins from left to right and tries to pick the most selective join first—meaning the table with the fewest rows that match the join condition. However, in complex queries, the optimizer may not always make the best choice, particularly if the join order results in large intermediate result sets. In such cases, manually reordering the joins or breaking the query into smaller subqueries can help reduce the number of rows processed at each step, leading to better performance.

Another strategy for optimizing join performance is to reduce the number of rows involved in the join. The more data that needs to be joined, the more work the database engine must do. Therefore, it is important to filter the data as early as possible in the query execution process. One way to achieve this is by using appropriate WHERE conditions to limit the rows retrieved from each table before performing the join. By reducing the number of rows in the join operation, the database engine can perform the join more efficiently, minimizing the amount of data that needs to be processed. For example, applying a WHERE clause to filter out irrelevant rows from the tables before the join can significantly speed up the query.

Using subqueries can also help optimize join performance in certain cases. Instead of joining multiple large tables directly, subqueries can be used to limit the data from each table before performing the join. By running subqueries independently and then joining their results, the database can reduce the number of rows that need to be processed in the final join. Subqueries can be particularly useful when joining tables with different levels of data granularity or when working with highly filtered data. However, subqueries can also introduce additional complexity and overhead, so they should be used carefully and only when they provide a clear performance benefit.

The use of derived tables is another technique that can improve join performance. A derived table is essentially a temporary table created as part of the query execution. It is defined within the query itself and can be used to store intermediate results before performing the join. By using derived tables, DBAs can break down complex queries into smaller, more manageable pieces, allowing for more efficient joins. For example, if a query involves joining three or more tables with complex conditions, creating derived tables to store the results of the first few joins can help reduce the size of the intermediate results, making the subsequent join operations faster.

Another important factor in optimizing joins is the choice of join algorithms used by MySQL and MariaDB. The database engine employs various algorithms to execute joins, with the most common being nested loop joins, sort-merge joins, and hash joins. In a nested loop join, the database scans one table and for each row, searches the other table for matching rows. This can be efficient when joining small tables, but can lead to poor performance when dealing with large datasets. Sort-merge joins are used when both tables are sorted on the join columns, and the database can merge the two sorted tables to find matching rows. This is generally more efficient than nested loop joins for large datasets, but it requires sorting the tables first. Hash joins are used when the join columns are not sorted, and the database builds a hash table for one table and then probes it with the rows from the other table. Hash joins can be very efficient when there is no natural ordering of the data and when working with large datasets that are not indexed.

To further optimize join performance, MySQL and MariaDB support the use of optimizer hints. Optimizer hints allow DBAs to provide guidance to the query optimizer, instructing it to use a specific index or join order. While the query optimizer is generally good at choosing the most efficient execution plan, there are cases where manual intervention can lead to better performance. By using hints, DBAs can override the optimizer's decisions and force it to use indexes or join strategies that have been shown to improve performance for specific queries. However, optimizer hints should be used sparingly, as they can make the query plan more rigid and less adaptable to changes in the database or workload.

In complex queries, it is also important to consider the impact of query execution on memory and disk I/O. Joins that require sorting or large intermediate result sets can quickly consume memory and disk space, leading to slower performance. To mitigate this, DBAs can optimize the memory allocation for temporary tables, which are often used during joins that require sorting or grouping. By increasing the tmp_table_size and max_heap_table_size parameters, DBAs can allow larger temporary tables to be created in memory, reducing the need for disk-based temporary tables and improving performance.

By leveraging the right combination of indexing, query structure, and execution strategies, DBAs can optimize join performance in MySQL and MariaDB databases. Understanding the inner workings of joins, the types of algorithms used, and how to manage memory and disk I/O during query execution allows for fine-tuned optimizations. Complex queries, when properly optimized, can execute much faster, significantly improving the overall performance of the database and ensuring that it can handle large volumes of data efficiently.

Handling Locking and Concurrency in MySQL and MariaDB

Locking and concurrency control are essential aspects of database management that ensure data consistency and integrity while allowing multiple transactions to be processed simultaneously. In MySQL and MariaDB, locking mechanisms are employed to prevent data corruption caused by concurrent updates or reads. However, improper handling of locking can lead to performance bottlenecks, deadlocks, and reduced throughput. Understanding how locking works in MySQL and MariaDB, as well as the different types of locks and isolation levels available, is crucial for database administrators (DBAs) who want to optimize performance and maintain smooth operation in multi-user environments.

MySQL and MariaDB use a variety of locking mechanisms to manage concurrent access to data. The most common types of locks are row-level locks, table-level locks, and metadata locks. Row-level locks are the most granular form of locking and are typically used by the InnoDB storage engine, which supports transactions and ensures ACID compliance. Row-level locking allows multiple transactions to modify different rows of the same table simultaneously, without interfering with one another. This makes InnoDB highly suitable for environments with high concurrency, as it minimizes contention and allows for greater parallelism.

In contrast, table-level locks are coarser and prevent other transactions from accessing the entire table while one transaction is modifying it. Table-level locks are used by storage engines like MyISAM, which does not support row-level locking. While table-level locks are simpler to manage, they can lead to significant performance issues in high-concurrency environments, as transactions are forced to wait for the lock to be released. For example, when one transaction holds a table-level lock for a table, other transactions that need to read or write to the same table must wait until the lock is released, potentially causing delays and reducing overall throughput.

Metadata locks, on the other hand, are used to prevent schema changes during certain operations. These locks are automatically acquired by MySQL or MariaDB when operations that modify the schema, such as ALTER TABLE or CREATE INDEX, are executed. While metadata locks are important for maintaining consistency, they can also lead to blocking in some scenarios, especially if long-running queries are in progress at the same time as schema modifications. Understanding when and how metadata locks are acquired is key to preventing unnecessary delays and ensuring that schema changes do not block critical operations.

MySQL and MariaDB also support different transaction isolation levels, which define the degree to which one transaction's changes are visible to other transactions. The isolation level directly influences locking behavior and concurrency control. The four standard isolation levels defined by the SQL standard are READ UNCOMMITTED, READ COMMITTED, REPEATABLE READ, and SERIALIZABLE. Each of these isolation levels offers a different balance between concurrency and data consistency.

At the lowest level, READ UNCOMMITTED allows transactions to read uncommitted changes made by other transactions, which can result in "dirty reads." This level offers the highest concurrency but at the cost of potential data inconsistencies. READ COMMITTED prevents dirty reads by ensuring that a transaction can only read data that has been committed by other transactions. While this isolation level prevents dirty reads, it still allows for non-repeatable reads, meaning that a transaction might read the same row multiple times and get different values if another transaction modifies the data in between reads.

REPEATABLE READ, the default isolation level in MySQL and MariaDB, ensures that once a transaction reads a row, it will see the same value every time it reads that row, even if other transactions modify the data. This level prevents both dirty reads and non-repeatable reads, providing a higher degree of consistency. However, it can still allow phantom reads, where a transaction reads a set of rows that match a certain condition, but another transaction inserts or deletes rows that would affect the result set. The highest isolation level, SERIALIZABLE, eliminates all anomalies by ensuring that transactions are executed serially, as if they were processed one after the other. While this level offers the highest consistency, it also has the greatest impact on concurrency, as it can lead to significant blocking and contention.

In high-concurrency environments, deadlocks can occur when two or more transactions hold locks on resources that the other transactions need, creating a cycle of dependencies that prevents any of the transactions from proceeding. When MySQL or MariaDB detects a deadlock, it automatically resolves the issue by rolling back one of the transactions, allowing the others to continue. While this automatic deadlock detection is useful, it is still important to design transactions in a way that minimizes the chances of deadlocks occurring. One approach to reducing deadlocks is to ensure that transactions acquire locks in a consistent order. For example, if multiple transactions need to access the same set of tables, all transactions should acquire locks in the same sequence to prevent circular dependencies.

Another strategy for handling locking and concurrency is optimizing the length of transactions. Long-running transactions are more likely to cause contention for locks, as they hold locks on resources for an extended period, blocking other transactions from accessing those resources. By keeping transactions short and focused, DBAs can minimize the time that locks are held and reduce the chances of conflicts. Using smaller, more frequent transactions can help improve concurrency by allowing other transactions to acquire locks more quickly.

One way to minimize locking contention is to carefully design the database schema and indexes. Proper indexing can significantly reduce the number of rows that need to be locked, allowing queries to complete more quickly and reducing the time that locks are held. For example, by creating appropriate indexes on columns used in WHERE clauses, JOIN conditions, or ORDER BY clauses, DBAs can improve query performance and reduce the need for full table scans, which require locks on the entire table. Additionally, using appropriate data types and avoiding excessive locking on large tables can also improve concurrency.

Optimizing queries is another key aspect of handling locking and concurrency. Poorly optimized queries that involve unnecessary joins, subqueries, or complex filtering conditions can lead to long transaction times, increasing the likelihood of locking contention. By analyzing query execution plans using EXPLAIN, DBAs can identify inefficient queries and take steps to optimize them, such as by rewriting the queries, adding missing indexes, or simplifying the query logic. Reducing the number of rows processed and minimizing the complexity of joins and subqueries can help ensure that queries execute faster, reducing the time that locks are held and improving concurrency.

MySQL and MariaDB also offer tools for monitoring locking behavior and detecting performance bottlenecks. The SHOW ENGINE INNODB STATUS command provides detailed information about the InnoDB storage engine's internal state, including information about current locks, transactions, and deadlocks. Additionally, the INFORMATION_SCHEMA tables, such as INNODB_LOCKS and INNODB_LOCK_WAITS, can be queried to gather information about active locks and transactions. By regularly monitoring locking behavior, DBAs can identify potential issues and take proactive steps to optimize concurrency and prevent performance degradation.

Handling locking and concurrency in MySQL and MariaDB requires a thorough understanding of how the database engine manages locks, transactions, and isolation levels. By carefully managing transaction isolation, optimizing query execution, designing efficient schemas and indexes, and minimizing the duration of transactions, DBAs can ensure that MySQL and MariaDB databases perform efficiently even in high-concurrency environments. Understanding how to manage and optimize locking is key to maintaining high availability, preventing bottlenecks, and ensuring that database operations run smoothly under heavy loads.

Deadlock Detection and Resolution Strategies

Deadlocks are a common and challenging issue in relational databases, especially when multiple transactions are simultaneously trying to access the same resources, such as tables or rows, in conflicting ways. A deadlock occurs when two or more transactions are each waiting for the other to release a lock on a resource they need, resulting in a cycle of dependencies where none of the transactions can proceed. Deadlocks can significantly degrade the performance of a MySQL or MariaDB database, as transactions are blocked and resources remain locked. The ability to detect and resolve deadlocks efficiently is crucial for maintaining the performance and reliability of database systems in high-concurrency environments.

In MySQL and MariaDB, deadlocks typically occur when multiple transactions hold locks on resources that the other transactions need, and none of them can proceed. For example, Transaction A may hold a lock on Table 1 and wait for a lock on Table 2, while Transaction B holds a lock on Table 2 and waits for a lock on Table 1. In this scenario, neither transaction can proceed because they are each waiting for the other to release the lock. Deadlocks can also occur when a transaction locks rows in a different order compared to other transactions, creating circular dependencies between transactions. While deadlocks are inevitable in highly concurrent systems, it is important to have mechanisms in place to detect and resolve them quickly to minimize their impact on database performance.

MySQL and MariaDB use an automatic deadlock detection mechanism to identify when a deadlock occurs. When a deadlock is detected, the database engine will automatically choose one of the transactions involved in the deadlock and roll it back to allow the other transactions to proceed. This automatic resolution ensures that at least one of the transactions can be completed, and the other transactions can be retried once the locked resources are released. However, this automatic process does not prevent the deadlock from affecting overall performance, as the rolled-back transaction must be re-executed, leading to additional overhead.

To minimize the frequency and impact of deadlocks, DBAs should focus on several strategies, both in terms of query design and transaction management. One of the most effective strategies is ensuring that transactions acquire locks in a consistent order. When multiple transactions need to access the same set of tables, ensuring that all transactions acquire the locks in the same sequence can help prevent deadlocks from occurring. For example, if Transaction A acquires a lock on Table 1 and then on Table 2, Transaction B should also acquire the locks in the same order. This prevents circular dependencies and reduces the likelihood of deadlocks. Designing applications to follow a consistent locking order, particularly in environments with complex relationships between tables, can significantly reduce the chance of deadlocks.

Another important strategy for preventing deadlocks is keeping transactions as short as possible. Long-running transactions that hold locks for extended periods increase the risk of deadlocks because they prevent other transactions from acquiring the necessary locks. By reducing the duration of transactions, DBAs can minimize the time that locks are held, thereby reducing the chances of a deadlock occurring. Additionally, when possible, DBAs should ensure that transactions only lock the resources they need and release locks as soon as they are no longer required. This can be achieved by committing or rolling back transactions quickly and ensuring that long-running operations, such as complex updates or batch processing, are broken into smaller, more manageable transactions.

Optimizing queries to reduce the amount of data being locked can also help reduce the likelihood of deadlocks. Queries that involve full table scans or large range scans can increase the chances of deadlocks, especially in systems with many concurrent transactions. By ensuring that queries are properly indexed and that only the necessary rows are locked, DBAs can help prevent unnecessary lock contention. For example, when updating rows in a large table, using an index that allows the database to quickly identify the rows that need to be updated can prevent the need to lock large portions of the table. Similarly, using more selective WHERE clauses can help minimize the number of rows affected by a query, reducing the scope of the locks and minimizing the potential for deadlocks.

Deadlocks can also be influenced by the isolation level of transactions. In MySQL and MariaDB, the default isolation level is REPEATABLE READ, which ensures that once a transaction reads a row, it will always see the same value for that row throughout the duration of the transaction. While this isolation level prevents many types of data anomalies, such as dirty reads and non-repeatable reads, it can also increase the likelihood of deadlocks in certain situations. For example, transactions that involve multiple updates to the same set of rows can cause conflicts if they hold locks on the same rows for extended periods. In some cases, using a lower isolation level, such as READ COMMITTED, can reduce the chances of deadlocks by allowing transactions to release locks more quickly. However, reducing the isolation level may introduce other consistency issues, so it should be used carefully and based on the specific requirements of the application.

MySQL and MariaDB provide several tools for monitoring deadlocks and understanding their causes. The SHOW ENGINE INNODB STATUS command provides detailed information about the state of the InnoDB storage engine, including information about deadlocks that have occurred. This command displays a snapshot of the last detected deadlock, including the transactions involved, the locks they held, and the SQL statements they were executing. By analyzing this information, DBAs can identify patterns in deadlocks and make informed decisions about how to resolve them. Additionally, the INFORMATION_SCHEMA tables, such as INNODB_LOCKS and INNODB_LOCK_WAITS, can be queried to gather real-time information about active locks and transactions, helping to identify potential deadlock scenarios before they occur.

Once a deadlock is detected, resolving it requires carefully considering the impact of rolling back transactions. Since MySQL and MariaDB automatically roll back one of the transactions involved in the deadlock, the DBAs need to decide which transaction to prioritize for rollback. In most cases, it is best to roll back the transaction that has made the least progress or the one that is the easiest to restart. However, in some cases, the application may need to be modified to handle deadlocks more gracefully, such as by retrying transactions that are rolled back or using application-level retry logic to ensure that operations are not permanently interrupted by deadlocks.

Additionally, implementing proper error handling and retry mechanisms in the application can help mitigate the impact of deadlocks. When a transaction is rolled back due to a deadlock, the application can catch the error, handle it appropriately, and attempt to re-execute the transaction. This ensures that the database remains responsive and that critical operations are not permanently blocked by deadlocks. By implementing such strategies, DBAs can reduce the operational impact of deadlocks and ensure that the database continues to function smoothly, even under high concurrency.

Deadlock detection and resolution are essential for maintaining the performance and reliability of MySQL and MariaDB databases, particularly in environments with high concurrency. By following best practices for transaction design, query optimization, and error handling, DBAs can minimize the occurrence of deadlocks and ensure that their systems continue to run efficiently. While deadlocks cannot be entirely avoided, the right strategies and tools can help detect and resolve them quickly, ensuring that database operations remain smooth and that resources are used effectively.

Query Cache Management and Best Practices

Query caching is a powerful optimization technique in MySQL and MariaDB that can significantly improve performance by reducing the time required to execute frequently run queries. When enabled, query caching stores the results of SELECT statements in memory, so that when the same query is executed again, the database engine can retrieve the results directly from the cache rather than re-executing the query and accessing the underlying data. This can lead to a significant reduction in response times, especially for read-heavy workloads, where the same queries are executed repeatedly. However, while query caching can provide substantial benefits, it must be carefully managed to avoid performance degradation and inefficiencies, especially in write-heavy environments.

The query cache in MySQL and MariaDB works by caching the result set of a query in memory. When a query is executed, the database engine first checks if the query result is already cached. If it is, the cached result is returned to the client without the need for further processing. If the query result is not cached or the cache has been invalidated, the database engine executes the query, stores the result in the cache, and then returns the result to the client. This caching mechanism can significantly speed up repeated queries, especially when the underlying data does not change frequently. In read-heavy environments, where the same queries are executed multiple times, the query cache can lead to large performance gains by eliminating redundant query execution.

However, query caching is not always beneficial, and in some cases, it can even cause performance issues. The primary challenge with query cache is that it must be invalidated whenever the data in the underlying table changes. For example, when an INSERT, UPDATE, or DELETE operation is performed on a table, the query cache for any queries that depend on that table must be cleared. This invalidation process can lead to overhead, particularly in write-heavy environments, where the cache is frequently cleared and rebuilt. In such environments, the performance benefits of query caching are diminished, as the cache is often empty or invalidated before it can be used. This is why query cache is most effective in environments where read operations far outweigh write operations.

To manage the query cache effectively, it is essential to understand and configure the relevant cache parameters. The query_cache_size parameter defines the total amount of memory allocated to the query cache. A larger cache allows more results to be stored, potentially reducing the need to execute queries repeatedly. However, allocating too much memory to the query cache can lead to resource contention and cause other processes, such as the InnoDB buffer pool, to suffer from a lack of memory. DBAs must balance the size of the query cache with the overall memory requirements of the database system. The query_cache_limit parameter controls the maximum size of individual query results that can be cached. Setting this parameter appropriately ensures that large result sets are not cached unnecessarily, which could waste memory and reduce the efficiency of the cache.

Another important parameter is query_cache_type, which controls whether query caching is enabled, disabled, or only applied to certain queries. By default, MySQL and MariaDB cache SELECT statements that do not include any conditions that would make the results variable, such as LIMIT or ORDER BY clauses. The query_cache_type parameter allows DBAs to configure whether the cache is used for all queries, no queries, or only for queries that meet certain criteria. In some cases, it may be beneficial to disable the query cache entirely, especially in systems with high write activity or where caching does not provide significant performance benefits.

Proper management of the query cache also involves understanding when cache invalidation occurs. Each time a write operation modifies the data in a table, any query results dependent on that table are invalidated and must be recomputed. This invalidation process can become a bottleneck if many queries depend on the same set of data and the underlying data changes frequently. To reduce the frequency of invalidation, DBAs can optimize the design of queries to limit the impact of data modifications. For example, using more selective queries or breaking larger queries into smaller parts can help limit the amount of data affected by each write operation, thus reducing the number of queries that need to be invalidated. Additionally, avoiding unnecessary write operations that impact large portions of the database can help keep the query cache more stable.

One of the challenges with query caching is that not all queries benefit from it. Simple queries with few parameters, such as basic SELECT statements that retrieve a small number of rows from a table, are more likely to be cached effectively. However, more complex queries, such as those that involve joins, aggregations, or large result sets, may not cache well because their results may be too large or vary too frequently. In such cases, the overhead of caching and invalidation may outweigh the performance benefits of caching. Additionally, queries that rely on user-specific or session-specific data, such as those that involve user input or session variables, cannot be cached effectively, as the results will vary depending on the user's input. In these cases, caching at the application level, using tools like Memcached or Redis, may be more effective for improving performance.

To further optimize query cache performance, DBAs can monitor the effectiveness of the cache using the SHOW STATUS command, which provides statistics about cache hits, misses, and invalidations. The Qcache_hits variable indicates the number of times the cache was successfully used, while the Qcache_inserts variable shows how often a query result was inserted into the cache. The Qcache_lowmem_prunes variable indicates how many times the cache was cleared due to memory pressure. By examining these statistics, DBAs can identify whether the query cache is being used effectively and adjust cache parameters as needed to maximize performance.

Another important consideration for query cache management is handling concurrency. In a multi-user environment, many queries may be attempting to access the cache simultaneously, leading to contention for cache resources. To address this, MySQL and MariaDB use a lock to synchronize access to the query cache. However, this lock can become a bottleneck in high-concurrency environments, especially when there are frequent writes or cache invalidations. To minimize this contention, DBAs can fine-tune other database parameters, such as the innodb_buffer_pool_size or max_connections, to ensure that there is enough memory and system resources to handle the load. In some cases, DBAs may also choose to disable query caching in favor of other caching strategies, such as caching at the application level or using an external caching layer like Memcached or Redis.

In addition to optimizing query cache usage, it is important to regularly clean up stale or unused cache entries to prevent the cache from becoming bloated and inefficient. MySQL and MariaDB automatically remove expired or invalidated cache entries, but DBAs should ensure that the cache size is balanced with the available memory to avoid wasting resources. In high-traffic systems, the cache can fill up quickly, and it is crucial to ensure that only frequently used queries are kept in memory, while less useful data is evicted.

Effective query cache management requires understanding the workload and query patterns of the database. By carefully tuning cache parameters, monitoring cache performance, and applying best practices for data modification and query design, DBAs can ensure that the query cache provides maximum performance benefits without introducing unnecessary overhead. In some cases, query caching may not be appropriate, and other strategies, such as application-level caching or index optimization, may be more effective. By leveraging the right caching techniques for the specific workload, DBAs can significantly enhance the performance and scalability of MySQL and MariaDB databases.

Tuning the InnoDB Buffer Pool for Maximum Efficiency

The InnoDB buffer pool is a critical component of MySQL and MariaDB databases, responsible for caching data and indexes in memory to reduce the need for disk I/O. Optimizing the InnoDB buffer pool is essential for achieving high performance, particularly in systems with large datasets or high read-write activity. When configured correctly, the buffer pool allows the database to operate at peak efficiency by minimizing the latency associated with accessing data stored on disk. Given the importance of the buffer pool, understanding how it works and how to properly tune it for your specific workload is crucial for database administrators (DBAs) looking to maximize the performance of their MySQL or MariaDB databases.

At its core, the InnoDB buffer pool is a region of memory allocated by MySQL or MariaDB to store data and index pages from InnoDB tables. The primary function of the buffer pool is to keep the most frequently accessed data in memory, so that subsequent read operations can be serviced quickly without having to access the disk. This significantly improves the performance of queries, as reading data from memory is orders of magnitude faster than reading it from disk. Additionally, the buffer pool stores InnoDB indexes, which helps speed up query execution by allowing for faster lookups of indexed columns.

Tuning the InnoDB buffer pool involves configuring the size of the buffer pool, which determines how much memory will be allocated for caching. The buffer pool size should be large enough to hold a significant portion of the working dataset in memory, but not so large that it consumes all available system memory, leaving insufficient resources for other processes. A common recommendation is to allocate between 60% and 80% of the available system memory to the InnoDB buffer pool on dedicated database servers. However, the optimal size depends on the specific workload, the size of the dataset, and the available system resources. In environments with very large datasets, DBAs may need to adjust the buffer pool size to ensure that the most frequently accessed data is kept in memory while avoiding system memory exhaustion.

To configure the size of the InnoDB buffer pool, the innodb_buffer_pool_size parameter is used. This parameter controls the amount of memory allocated to the buffer pool, and DBAs should set it based on the available system memory and the size of the working set. The working set refers to the subset of data that is frequently accessed and is most likely to benefit from being cached in memory. If the buffer pool is too small, the database will frequently need to read data from disk, which can result in slower query performance. On the other hand, allocating too much memory to the buffer pool can lead to memory pressure, causing the operating system to swap memory to disk, which can degrade overall system performance.

For systems with large amounts of memory, it may be beneficial to configure multiple buffer pool instances. The innodb_buffer_pool_instances parameter controls how many instances of the buffer pool are created. By splitting the buffer pool into multiple instances, MySQL or MariaDB can better utilize multi-core processors and reduce contention between threads accessing the buffer pool. This is particularly useful for systems with a large number of CPU cores, as it allows multiple threads to access different portions of the buffer pool concurrently. The optimal number of buffer pool instances depends on the number of available CPU cores and the amount of memory allocated to the buffer pool. Typically, it is recommended to set the number of buffer pool instances to the number of CPU cores or a multiple of it for large, multi-core systems.

In addition to configuring the buffer pool size and instances, DBAs should also consider the innodb_buffer_pool_dump_at_shutdown and innodb_buffer_pool_load_at_startup parameters. These parameters control the behavior of the buffer pool during server startup and shutdown. When innodb_buffer_pool_dump_at_shutdown is enabled, the contents of the buffer pool are saved to disk at shutdown. This allows the database to load the cached data back into memory when it starts up again, reducing the time required to warm up the buffer pool after a restart. Similarly, the innodb_buffer_pool_load_at_startup parameter determines whether the buffer pool is loaded from disk at startup. Enabling these options can help improve startup times, especially for large databases, by avoiding the need to load data from disk into memory during the initial query executions.

Another important factor to consider when tuning the InnoDB buffer pool is the InnoDB flush method. The innodb_flush_method parameter controls how InnoDB writes data to disk, and it can have a significant impact on both performance and durability. The default flush method, fsync, writes data to disk in a traditional manner, ensuring durability by flushing data to disk at each commit. However, for systems with high-performance storage, such as solid-state drives (SSDs), the O_DIRECT flush method may offer better performance by bypassing the operating system's file system cache. Using O_DIRECT can help reduce double caching, as data will not be cached in both the operating system cache and the InnoDB buffer pool, leading to more efficient I/O operations. However, using O_DIRECT may require careful tuning of other system parameters, such as the filesystem and disk I/O configuration.

Another crucial parameter related to buffer pool performance is innodb_io_capacity, which controls the number of I/O operations InnoDB will perform per second. This setting determines the rate at which InnoDB flushes data to disk, and it can be adjusted to match the performance characteristics of the underlying storage system. For systems with high-performance storage devices, such as SSDs, increasing the innodb_io_capacity value can help improve write throughput and reduce latency. Conversely, on systems with slower disks, reducing the innodb_io_capacity value may prevent excessive disk I/O and ensure more consistent performance.

It is also important to monitor the performance of the InnoDB buffer pool and make adjustments as needed. MySQL and MariaDB provide several status variables that can be used to track buffer pool usage, including innodb_buffer_pool_reads, innodb_buffer_pool_hits, and innodb_buffer_pool_wait_free. These variables provide insights into how effectively the buffer pool is being utilized, such as the number of reads that were serviced from the buffer pool versus those that required disk access. By analyzing these metrics, DBAs can determine whether the buffer pool size needs to be adjusted or if additional optimizations are required. A high rate of buffer pool reads or buffer pool waits indicates that the buffer pool may be too small, while low buffer pool hit rates suggest that the data is not being cached efficiently.

One additional aspect of buffer pool tuning is the management of the InnoDB adaptive hash index, which is an internal structure that helps speed up lookups for frequently accessed data. The adaptive hash index stores hashes of indexed rows, allowing InnoDB to quickly locate rows without having to scan the entire index. By default, the adaptive hash index is enabled, but in some cases, disabling it or adjusting its parameters may improve performance. For example, on systems with a large buffer pool or in environments with complex query patterns, the adaptive hash index may introduce overhead by consuming memory and causing unnecessary contention. DBAs should monitor the performance of the adaptive hash index and make adjustments based on their workload and system configuration.

Tuning the InnoDB buffer pool is essential for optimizing the performance of MySQL and MariaDB databases. By configuring the buffer pool size, instances, and related parameters appropriately, DBAs can ensure that the database operates efficiently, with minimal reliance on disk I/O. Regular monitoring of buffer pool performance and fine-tuning of related parameters, such as the flush method and I/O capacity, helps ensure that the buffer pool remains effective even as the database workload evolves. Ultimately, proper buffer pool tuning can lead to faster query performance, reduced disk latency, and a more responsive database, all of which contribute to the overall performance of MySQL and MariaDB systems.

Best Practices for Handling Large Datasets in MySQL and MariaDB

Handling large datasets in MySQL and MariaDB presents several challenges that, if not addressed, can severely impact the performance, reliability, and scalability of a database. As databases grow in size, the time required to query, update, and manage the data increases, and without proper optimization, queries can become sluggish and resource consumption can rise significantly. Best practices for managing large datasets involve a combination of database architecture decisions, query optimizations, storage engine configurations, and maintenance strategies. By carefully implementing these best practices, database administrators (DBAs) can ensure that their MySQL and MariaDB systems can handle large volumes of data efficiently, even under high load.

One of the first and most important considerations when working with large datasets is the choice of storage engine. MySQL and MariaDB offer different storage engines, each with its own performance characteristics. InnoDB is the default and most commonly used storage engine due to its support for ACID-compliant transactions, foreign keys, and row-level locking. InnoDB's support for transactions and row-level locking makes it particularly suitable for large, transactional systems. However, for specific workloads, such as read-heavy environments, the MyISAM storage engine may provide better performance due to its simpler design and table-level locking. DBAs must carefully assess the nature of their workload to determine which storage engine is best suited for their needs. In general, InnoDB is recommended for most applications dealing with large datasets, especially when data integrity and concurrent access are important.

Once the storage engine is chosen, optimizing table structure and indexing becomes crucial. For large datasets, poorly designed tables and inefficient indexing can severely impact query performance. Indexing is one of the most effective ways to improve data retrieval speed, as it allows the database engine to quickly locate the rows that match a query's filtering conditions. However, creating too many indexes can have the opposite effect, as the database must spend additional time updating these indexes during insert, update, and delete operations. To strike the right balance, DBAs should analyze the query patterns and index only those columns that are frequently used in WHERE clauses, JOIN conditions, or ORDER BY clauses. Additionally, for large datasets, composite indexes (indexes on multiple columns) can be used to optimize queries that filter by several columns simultaneously. However, it is essential to carefully order the columns in composite indexes to align with how queries are typically structured.

Another key consideration when handling large datasets is partitioning. Partitioning allows a large table to be split into smaller, more manageable pieces, called partitions. Each partition stores a subset of the data, which can improve query performance by limiting the amount of data the database needs to scan. Partitioning can be done based on a variety of criteria, such as range partitioning (based on ranges of values, such as date ranges), list partitioning (based on specific values, such as geographic regions), or hash partitioning (evenly distributing rows across partitions using a hash function). By partitioning large tables, DBAs can ensure that queries only scan the relevant partitions, reducing I/O and speeding up query execution. Furthermore, partitioning can make maintenance tasks, such as backups or purging old data, more efficient, as individual partitions can be backed up or archived without affecting the entire table.

When dealing with large datasets, query optimization is paramount. Inefficient queries can quickly bring down the performance of a database. One of the first steps in optimizing queries for large datasets is ensuring that they are properly indexed. Queries that perform full table scans are particularly costly in terms of performance, as the database must read every row of the table to find matching records. Using EXPLAIN statements to analyze query execution plans can help identify whether a query is performing a table scan and whether indexes are being used effectively. For queries that involve complex joins or large result sets, DBAs can optimize the query structure by reducing the number of rows processed, breaking the query into smaller parts, or rewriting the query to make better use of available indexes.

In addition to indexing, denormalization can sometimes be a useful technique for optimizing queries on large datasets. Denormalization involves storing redundant data to reduce the need for complex joins in queries. While normalization reduces data redundancy and ensures data integrity, denormalization can improve performance by eliminating the need to join multiple tables in queries, which can be slow with large datasets. However, denormalization comes with trade-offs, as it increases storage requirements and can lead to data inconsistencies if not carefully managed. It should be used selectively and in cases where performance gains outweigh the potential downsides.

For large datasets, proper memory management is another critical aspect of ensuring good performance. MySQL and MariaDB provide several memory buffers that can be tuned to optimize query performance, such as the InnoDB buffer pool, which caches data and indexes in memory to reduce disk I/O. Increasing the size of the buffer pool allows the database to store more data in memory, reducing the need for disk reads and improving query performance. However, allocating too much memory to the buffer pool can cause the system to run out of resources, leading to swapping and degraded performance. As a rule of thumb, it is recommended to allocate 60% to 70% of system memory to the InnoDB buffer pool on dedicated database servers, but this should be adjusted based on the size of the dataset and available system resources.

Another way to handle large datasets efficiently is through the use of optimized storage hardware. As data volumes grow, disk I/O becomes a major bottleneck, particularly with traditional spinning hard drives (HDDs). Switching to solid-state drives (SSDs) can significantly improve I/O performance, as SSDs offer faster read and write speeds and lower latency. In high-performance environments, using RAID configurations, such as RAID 10, can further enhance disk performance by providing redundancy and improved data throughput. It is essential to ensure that the storage subsystem can handle the demands of the workload and that disk I/O is optimized for maximum efficiency.

Managing large datasets also involves ensuring that regular maintenance tasks, such as backups, indexing, and data purging, are performed efficiently. As data grows, the time required for these tasks can increase, so it is important to schedule them during low-traffic periods or use strategies like incremental backups to reduce the impact on database performance. Regularly optimizing tables and rebuilding indexes can also help improve performance by removing fragmentation and ensuring that indexes are efficient. Additionally, archiving old data and partitioning tables can help reduce the amount of data that needs to be processed during maintenance tasks, further improving overall database performance.

Finally, monitoring the database regularly is essential when working with large datasets. Using tools like MySQL Enterprise Monitor, Percona Monitoring and Management (PMM), or other third-party monitoring solutions can provide insights into query performance, resource utilization, and potential bottlenecks. By continuously monitoring the database and adjusting configurations as necessary, DBAs can ensure that the system remains responsive and efficient, even as the dataset grows.

Handling large datasets in MySQL and MariaDB requires a multi-faceted approach that includes optimizing the database schema, configuring storage engines, indexing effectively, partitioning tables, and optimizing queries. Memory management, disk I/O optimization, and hardware considerations also play critical roles in ensuring that the database can handle large amounts of data efficiently. By implementing best practices and regularly monitoring the system, DBAs can maintain high performance and ensure that their MySQL and MariaDB databases are capable of scaling to meet the demands of large datasets.

Managing and Tuning Foreign Key Constraints

Foreign key constraints are an essential feature of relational databases that ensure data integrity by enforcing relationships between tables. In MySQL and MariaDB, foreign keys allow one table to reference another, ensuring that the data in related tables is consistent and accurate. However, managing and tuning foreign key constraints effectively is crucial for maintaining both data integrity and performance. While foreign keys help enforce referential integrity, they can also introduce performance overhead, particularly in systems with large datasets or high write operations. Understanding how to manage and optimize foreign key constraints is key for database administrators (DBAs) seeking to balance data integrity with optimal performance.

The primary function of foreign key constraints is to ensure that values in a child table correspond to valid entries in a parent table. For example, if a "orders" table references a "customers" table via a customer_id column, the foreign key constraint ensures that any value inserted into the customer_id column of the orders table must already exist in the customer_id column of the customers table. This helps prevent orphaned records, where a child table references data that does not exist in the parent table, thus preserving the integrity of the database.

When working with foreign key constraints in MySQL and MariaDB, it is important to understand the various options for handling updates and deletions of data in the parent table. By default, foreign key constraints enforce two key actions: ON DELETE and ON UPDATE. These actions determine what happens to the rows in the child table when corresponding rows in the parent table are deleted or updated. For example, the ON DELETE CASCADE option will automatically delete any rows in the child table that reference a deleted row in the parent table. Similarly, ON UPDATE CASCADE ensures that updates to the parent table's primary key are reflected in the child table's corresponding foreign key values. While cascading actions can simplify data management, they can also lead to performance overhead if not used carefully, particularly when dealing with large tables or complex relationships.

For systems with high write operations, it is often beneficial to consider alternative actions such as ON DELETE SET NULL or ON DELETE RESTRICT. The ON DELETE SET NULL option will set the foreign key column in the child table to NULL when the corresponding parent row is deleted, which can help avoid cascading deletes that affect multiple rows in the child table. However, this option requires that the foreign key column in the child table allows NULL values, and it may introduce additional complexity if there are other constraints or indexes that depend on non-NULL values. The ON DELETE RESTRICT option prevents the deletion of a row in the parent table if any rows in the child table reference it, thereby ensuring that data in the child table remains intact. While ON DELETE RESTRICT prevents unwanted deletions, it can lead to blocking behavior if there are many references to the parent row in the child table, as the parent row cannot be deleted until the child rows are handled.

One of the most critical performance considerations when managing foreign key constraints is the impact of indexing. In MySQL and MariaDB, foreign key columns must be indexed to enforce the integrity of the foreign key relationship efficiently. Without proper indexes, foreign key operations can be slow, as the database must perform a full table scan to check for matching values in the parent table. Indexing the foreign key column in the child table improves performance by allowing the database to quickly locate matching rows in the parent table, reducing the overhead of checking referential integrity. Additionally, indexing the primary key column in the parent table is also essential for ensuring efficient lookups when foreign key checks are performed. While foreign keys automatically create an index on the child table's foreign key column, DBAs should verify that the indexing strategy is appropriate for their workload and may need to create additional indexes to optimize query performance.

Another important aspect of managing foreign key constraints is the use of transactional consistency. In MySQL and MariaDB, foreign key checks are performed within the context of a transaction. When a transaction is committed, the database engine ensures that all foreign key constraints are satisfied, and any changes made to the parent or child tables are reflected in the database. This transactional consistency ensures that the database remains in a valid state, even if a transaction is rolled back. However, the enforcement of foreign key constraints can introduce additional overhead, particularly in systems with high transaction rates. DBAs should ensure that transactions are as short as possible to reduce the time foreign key checks are held, thus minimizing the potential impact on other transactions. Additionally, when using foreign keys with InnoDB, it is important to ensure that the database is using the correct isolation level to prevent issues such as dirty reads or phantom reads, which could cause foreign key checks to fail or behave inconsistently.

The choice of storage engine plays a crucial role in the performance of foreign key constraints. InnoDB is the only storage engine in MySQL and MariaDB that fully supports foreign key constraints. Other storage engines, such as MyISAM, do not support foreign keys, which can lead to data integrity issues in applications that require relational consistency. While InnoDB provides excellent support for foreign keys, it is important to understand that enforcing foreign key constraints incurs some performance overhead. This overhead is particularly noticeable in systems with high write operations, as every INSERT, UPDATE, or DELETE operation that affects a foreign key must be validated to ensure that the integrity of the relationship is maintained. For systems that require high write throughput, DBAs should carefully assess the trade-offs between enforcing foreign key constraints and maintaining performance.

To mitigate the performance impact of foreign key constraints, DBAs can implement several optimization strategies. One approach is to use batch inserts or updates when possible, which reduces the number of foreign key checks required during individual transactions. Instead of performing multiple single-row INSERTs or UPDATEs, batch operations can group many changes into a single transaction, reducing the frequency of foreign key validation. Additionally, foreign key checks can be temporarily disabled during bulk data loading operations using the SET foreign_key_checks = 0; command. However, disabling foreign key checks should be done cautiously, as it can lead to data integrity violations if the data being inserted does not adhere to the constraints.

Another useful strategy for managing foreign key constraints is to break up large tables with complex relationships into smaller, more manageable partitions. Partitioning can help reduce the number of rows that need to be checked when enforcing foreign key constraints, improving the performance of related queries. Partitioning also allows for more efficient data management, as individual partitions can be backed up, archived, or purged independently, reducing the impact on the entire table.

Regular monitoring of foreign key performance is essential to ensure that foreign key constraints do not become a bottleneck. Tools like the MySQL Enterprise Monitor, Percona Monitoring and Management (PMM), and other third-party monitoring solutions can provide insights into foreign key operations, including how frequently foreign key checks are performed and the time spent enforcing these constraints. By analyzing this data, DBAs can identify potential performance issues related to foreign key constraints and take proactive steps to address them.

Managing and tuning foreign key constraints in MySQL and MariaDB is a balancing act between maintaining data integrity and ensuring high performance. By carefully configuring foreign key actions, optimizing indexing, and utilizing transaction management techniques, DBAs can ensure that their databases remain both consistent and efficient. As databases grow in size and complexity, it is essential to continuously evaluate and optimize the performance of foreign key constraints to meet the needs of the workload. With the right strategies in place, foreign key constraints can be used effectively without sacrificing database performance.

Replication Tuning for Performance and Reliability

Replication is a fundamental feature in MySQL and MariaDB that allows data to be copied from one server (the master) to one or more other servers (the slaves). It is often used for creating redundant copies of data, distributing read queries, and enhancing data availability and fault tolerance. Replication can improve the performance and reliability of a database system by offloading read queries to replica servers, providing automatic failover in case of master server failure, and supporting data redundancy. However, to achieve optimal performance and reliability, replication must be properly tuned and managed. This chapter explores various strategies and best practices for tuning MySQL and MariaDB replication to enhance both performance and reliability.

One of the first considerations in replication tuning is the configuration of the replication threads. MySQL and MariaDB use multiple threads for replication: one for reading changes from the master (I/O thread) and another for applying those changes to the slave (SQL thread). The performance of these threads is critical for ensuring that replication remains fast and up-to-date. The I/O thread pulls binary log data from the master server and writes it to the relay log on the slave, while the SQL thread reads the relay log and applies the changes to the slave's data. For systems with high replication traffic or large datasets, it is important to ensure that the I/O and SQL threads can process the data efficiently. In high-throughput environments, DBAs should monitor these threads to ensure they are not lagging or encountering bottlenecks. Adjusting the innodb_flush_log_at_trx_commit parameter on the slave, for example, can help to reduce disk I/O and improve replication performance by controlling when transaction logs are flushed to disk.

Another important factor in replication tuning is the configuration of the replication delay. Replication lag occurs when the slave server falls behind the master due to slow processing of changes. This can happen if the slave server is overloaded, network latency is high, or the replication threads are not able to keep up with the volume of changes. DBAs should monitor replication lag using the SHOW SLAVE STATUS command, which provides information about the current position of the slave in the master's binary log. If replication lag becomes significant, it can lead to inconsistencies between the master and slave, resulting in outdated or missing data on the replica. One way to reduce replication lag is by optimizing the replication workload. For example, reducing the complexity of the queries executed on the master or limiting the number of writes can help ensure that the replication threads have enough capacity to keep up. Additionally, increasing the performance of the slave server by optimizing its hardware resources, such as upgrading to faster disk storage or adding more CPU cores, can help alleviate lag.

Network performance plays a crucial role in replication performance. Since replication relies on copying data from the master to the slave, network latency and bandwidth can significantly affect the replication speed. In high-traffic environments, a high-speed network connection between the master and slave servers is essential for minimizing replication lag and ensuring fast data transmission. For geographically distributed replication setups, where the master and slave servers are located in different regions, network latency can increase, leading to slower replication performance. In such cases, configuring replication to use compressed binary logs (by enabling the --log-bin-compress option) can help reduce the amount of data transmitted over the network, improving replication performance. Another strategy is to implement semi-synchronous replication, where the master waits for acknowledgment from at least one slave before committing a transaction. This can improve data consistency across replicas but may introduce slight delays. It is essential to carefully evaluate the trade-offs between consistency and performance when configuring replication for geographically distributed setups.

Replication also requires tuning for handling large transactions and high write loads. Large transactions on the master can cause delays in replication if the slave is not able to process the changes quickly enough. In such cases, DBAs can consider breaking large transactions into smaller, more manageable ones to reduce the load on the replication process. Additionally, enabling the --sync-binlog option on the master server can help ensure that binary logs are written and flushed to disk synchronously, preventing data loss in case of a crash. However, this can increase the load on the master and may affect its overall performance, so it is important to balance this option with the available system resources and workload requirements.

For better replication reliability, monitoring and automatic failover mechanisms are essential. Replication should not only be tuned for performance but also for high availability. Failover processes need to be in place in case the master server becomes unavailable. Tools such as MySQL Router, MHA (Master High Availability), and Orchestrator can be configured to detect a failure and automatically promote a slave to the master role, minimizing downtime. However, automatic failover can introduce its own challenges, such as ensuring data consistency and handling transactions that were in progress at the time of failure. Therefore, it is crucial to implement these mechanisms with proper safeguards, such as ensuring that the promoted slave has fully caught up with the master before it is promoted, and ensuring that any incomplete transactions are either rolled back or retried.

In addition to automatic failover, it is important to consider replication topology. The simplest replication setup involves a single master and one or more slaves. However, as the system grows, it may become necessary to implement more complex replication topologies, such as master-master or multi-master replication, where multiple master servers can handle both read and write operations. This setup can improve write scalability by distributing the write load across multiple servers. However, multi-master replication requires careful conflict resolution, as updates to the same data on different masters can lead to inconsistencies. Conflict resolution mechanisms, such as using timestamps or version numbers, can be employed to ensure data consistency across the masters. Alternatively, sharding can be implemented to split data across multiple masters, further enhancing scalability.

Monitoring replication health is another critical aspect of maintaining performance and reliability. DBAs should regularly monitor replication metrics such as the status of replication threads, replication lag, and any errors that may occur during replication. Tools like Percona Monitoring and Management (PMM), MySQL Enterprise Monitor, or custom scripts can be used to track replication performance and alert DBAs to any issues. Setting up regular backups and ensuring that replication is consistently up-to-date is also critical to avoid data loss in case of failures.

MySQL and MariaDB replication tuning also requires proper management of binary logs. Binary logs store all changes to the database and are used to propagate those changes to the slave servers. The binlog_cache_size parameter controls the size of the buffer used for storing changes before they are written to the binary log. Increasing this size can improve replication performance by reducing the number of writes to the binary log, particularly in systems with large transactions. However, increasing the binary log cache size can also increase memory usage, so it should be configured based on the system's available resources.

Replication in MySQL and MariaDB is a powerful feature that can improve both performance and reliability when configured correctly. By tuning various parameters such as replication threads, binary logs, and network settings, DBAs can optimize replication for both speed and consistency. Proper monitoring and failover mechanisms are essential to ensuring that replication remains reliable in high-availability environments. When tuned effectively, MySQL and MariaDB replication can scale efficiently, providing redundancy, distributing workloads, and improving the overall performance of the system.

Optimizing Master-Slave Replication Latency

Master-slave replication is a powerful feature in MySQL and MariaDB that provides data redundancy, scalability, and improved read performance by replicating data from a master server to one or more slave servers. However, as the system grows, managing and reducing replication latency becomes crucial to ensure data consistency and minimize the delay between the master and slave servers. Replication latency occurs when changes made on the master are not immediately reflected on the slave, leading to a lag in data availability. This delay can be problematic for applications that require real-time data consistency across servers. Optimizing master-slave replication latency involves understanding the factors that contribute to latency and implementing strategies to minimize these delays.

One of the primary causes of replication latency is the time it takes for data to be transmitted from the master to the slave. Replication involves several steps: the master writes changes to the binary log, the slave reads the binary log, and then the slave applies those changes to its data. Each of these steps introduces some delay, and any performance bottleneck at any point in the process can increase latency. The I/O thread on the slave is responsible for reading the binary log from the master, and the SQL thread is responsible for applying the changes to the slave's data. If either of these threads experiences a delay, replication lag can occur.

To optimize replication latency, the first step is ensuring that the master and slave servers are well-configured and capable of handling the replication load. The I/O thread on the slave must be able to efficiently read data from the master's binary log, while the SQL thread must be able to apply changes quickly. Both threads are dependent on the system's hardware, including CPU, memory, and disk I/O. For systems with high replication traffic, having adequate resources to handle both the master's write load and the slave's read load is critical. Ensuring that the slave has sufficient CPU power, fast disk I/O, and enough memory to handle the incoming data without causing bottlenecks can greatly reduce replication latency.

Network bandwidth and latency also play a significant role in replication performance. In geographically distributed setups, where the master and slave servers are located in different data centers, network latency can become a significant factor contributing to replication lag. High network latency can delay the transmission of the binary log from the master to the slave, exacerbating the replication delay. One way to mitigate this issue is by optimizing the network configuration between the master and slave, ensuring that there is sufficient bandwidth for the replication traffic. In some cases, using a dedicated network for replication can help reduce network congestion and improve replication speed. Additionally, employing techniques like compression for the binary log can reduce the amount of data transmitted over the network, further improving replication performance.

Another important consideration is the configuration of the replication threads themselves. By default, MySQL and MariaDB use a single I/O thread to read the binary log and a single SQL thread to apply the changes. While this is sufficient for smaller systems, it can become a bottleneck in high-traffic environments. To improve replication performance, DBAs can consider using multi-threaded replication, which allows multiple SQL threads to apply changes in parallel, reducing the time required to process the replication data. Multi-threaded replication can significantly improve replication performance in systems with many slave servers or high write traffic. However, multi-threaded replication requires careful configuration to ensure that changes are applied in the correct order, as MySQL and MariaDB apply transactions to the slave in the order in which they appear in the binary log.

Additionally, optimizing the master's write performance can help reduce the impact of replication latency. If the master is unable to process write requests quickly, it will generate a backlog of changes that need to be replicated to the slaves, resulting in increased replication lag. Ensuring that the master server is properly tuned to handle the write workload efficiently can help reduce the delay between the master and slave. Optimizing the database schema, queries, and indexes on the master can help ensure that write operations are fast and efficient, reducing the time required to generate binary log entries. Additionally, enabling asynchronous commits on the master can help improve write performance by reducing the time required to confirm transactions, although this comes at the cost of data durability in case of a crash.

In some cases, replication lag may occur due to the load on the slave server. The SQL thread on the slave applies changes from the binary log to the slave's data, and this process can be resource-intensive, especially if the slave is handling a large number of changes. To optimize this process, DBAs can configure the slave server to use multiple threads for applying changes, which can help distribute the load and reduce the time required to process changes. Additionally, reducing the complexity of the queries being replicated can help minimize the load on the SQL thread. For example, avoiding large or complex transactions on the master can reduce the amount of data that needs to be processed on the slave, improving replication speed.

Another factor that can contribute to replication latency is the use of semi-synchronous replication. In semi-synchronous replication, the master waits for at least one slave to acknowledge that it has received and written the changes to disk before committing the transaction. This ensures that the data is written to at least one slave, improving data durability and consistency. However, it also introduces a delay in replication, as the master must wait for the acknowledgment from the slave before continuing. To optimize semi-synchronous replication, DBAs can carefully evaluate the trade-offs between data consistency and replication performance. In environments where low replication latency is a priority, it may be beneficial to use asynchronous replication instead, although this comes with the risk of potential data inconsistency in the event of a failure.

To monitor replication latency effectively, DBAs should use tools such as the SHOW SLAVE STATUS command to track the status of replication on the slave. This command provides valuable information about the current replication position, including the replication lag, the status of the I/O and SQL threads, and any errors that may have occurred. By regularly monitoring these metrics, DBAs can identify potential issues and take corrective actions before they escalate. Setting up alerts to notify DBAs of significant replication lag can help ensure that the system remains healthy and that replication performance is optimized.

Replication lag is an inevitable aspect of large-scale database systems, but with careful tuning and optimization, DBAs can minimize its impact on performance. By configuring the replication threads, optimizing network performance, and tuning the master and slave servers, DBAs can significantly reduce replication latency. In systems with high replication traffic or geographically distributed replicas, multi-threaded replication, semi-synchronous replication, and other advanced techniques can further improve performance. Regular monitoring and maintenance are essential to ensure that replication continues to function smoothly, with minimal delays, and that the system remains responsive even under heavy load.

Setting Up and Tuning Galera Cluster for MariaDB

Galera Cluster for MariaDB is a powerful solution for achieving high availability and scalability in a MariaDB environment. It provides synchronous multi-master replication, allowing data to be written to any node in the cluster and ensuring that the data is automatically synchronized across all nodes. This makes Galera Cluster an ideal choice for applications that require real-time data consistency and high availability, as it ensures that all nodes in the cluster are always in sync. Setting up and tuning Galera Cluster requires careful planning and configuration to ensure optimal performance and reliability. In this chapter, we will explore the process of setting up and tuning a Galera Cluster for MariaDB to ensure that it performs efficiently and reliably under heavy load.

Setting up Galera Cluster for MariaDB begins with installing the necessary software on each node in the cluster. Galera is not a standalone software package; rather, it is integrated into MariaDB as a plugin. Therefore, you must ensure that you have a compatible version of MariaDB installed on all nodes. Galera Cluster supports several versions of MariaDB, but it is recommended to use the latest stable version to take advantage of the most recent features and improvements. Once MariaDB is installed, the Galera plugin can be enabled by modifying the configuration file (my.cnf) on each node. You must ensure that all nodes are using the same version of the Galera plugin, as compatibility issues can arise if the versions differ.

The next step in setting up a Galera Cluster is configuring the cluster parameters in the MariaDB configuration file. The most important parameter is wsrep_on, which enables the Galera replication functionality. By setting wsrep_on to ON, you are telling MariaDB to use Galera for replication. Additionally, you must configure the wsrep_cluster_address parameter, which specifies the address of the other nodes in the cluster. This allows each node to communicate with the others and form the cluster. The configuration of this parameter should include a comma-separated list of IP addresses or hostnames of the nodes in the cluster.

Another critical configuration parameter is wsrep_cluster_name, which is used to uniquely identify the Galera Cluster. All nodes in the cluster must have the same cluster name in their configuration files to be part of the same cluster. It is also important to configure the wsrep_node_address parameter, which specifies the address of the current node in the cluster. This is particularly important when setting up a new node, as it ensures that the node can join the correct cluster.

Once the basic cluster configuration is in place, you must configure the synchronization and replication settings. The wsrep_provider parameter specifies the path to the Galera library, and wsrep_sst_method controls the state transfer method used when nodes join the cluster. State Snapshot Transfer (SST) is the process by which a new node is brought up to date with the rest of the cluster. The most common SST method is xtrabackup, which is used to copy data from the donor node to the joining node. There are other SST methods available, such as rsync and mysqldump, but xtrabackup is generally recommended for its performance and reliability.

After configuring the basic settings, the next step is to tune the Galera Cluster to ensure optimal performance. One of the most important tuning parameters is wsrep_slave_threads, which controls the number of threads used to apply transactions on slave nodes. The default value is 4, but in high-traffic environments, you may need to increase this value to allow the slave nodes to process transactions more efficiently. Increasing the number of slave threads can improve replication performance, especially on nodes that handle heavy write loads. However, it is important to balance this value with the available resources, as setting it too high can lead to resource contention and reduced performance.

Another important tuning parameter is wsrep_max_ws_size, which controls the maximum size of the transactions that can be replicated. Large transactions can put significant pressure on the network and replication process, potentially causing delays and increasing latency. By setting a reasonable limit for wsrep_max_ws_size, you can ensure that large transactions are broken down into smaller, more manageable chunks. This can improve the performance of the replication process and reduce the likelihood of replication lag.

In addition to tuning the replication parameters, it is important to optimize the InnoDB settings on each node. Galera Cluster uses InnoDB as the storage engine, so the performance of InnoDB directly impacts the overall performance of the cluster. Key InnoDB parameters to consider include innodb_buffer_pool_size, innodb_log_file_size, and innodb_flush_log_at_trx_commit. The innodb_buffer_pool_size parameter controls the amount of memory allocated to the InnoDB buffer pool, which is used to cache data and indexes. Allocating sufficient memory to the buffer pool is crucial for ensuring that the database can handle a high volume of transactions and queries. For systems with large datasets, DBAs should allocate as much memory as possible to the buffer pool while leaving enough memory for other processes.

The innodb_log_file_size parameter controls the size of the InnoDB redo log files. Larger log files can improve performance by reducing the frequency of log file flushes, but they can also increase recovery time in the event of a crash. The innodb_flush_log_at_trx_commit parameter controls when the redo log is flushed to disk. Setting this value to 2 can reduce disk I/O and improve performance, but it comes with the risk of losing transactions in the event of a crash. It is essential to carefully consider the trade-offs between durability and performance when tuning these parameters.

One of the unique features of Galera Cluster is its ability to perform synchronous replication. While this ensures data consistency across all nodes, it can also introduce latency, especially in geographically distributed clusters. To minimize this latency, it is important to optimize the network connection between nodes. Low-latency, high-bandwidth connections are critical for maintaining replication performance in a Galera Cluster. In addition, you may want to consider using the wsrep_provider_options parameter to fine-tune Galera's internal behavior. For example, you can adjust the certification delay and flow control settings to control the rate at which transactions are applied across the cluster.

Monitoring the health and performance of the Galera Cluster is crucial to ensuring that it remains responsive and reliable. There are several tools available for monitoring Galera Cluster, including the built-in SHOW STATUS command in MariaDB, which provides valuable information about the cluster's state. Key metrics to monitor include the replication lag, the number of transactions pending in the queue, and the status of the nodes. Galera also provides several status variables, such as wsrep_cluster_size and wsrep_local_state, which can be used to track the health of the cluster and identify any potential issues.

Maintaining high availability in a Galera Cluster requires careful monitoring and proactive management. Galera is designed to automatically handle failover in the event of a node failure, but DBAs must ensure that proper failover mechanisms are in place to minimize downtime. Tools like Orchestrator can help automate the failover process by detecting node failures and promoting a new master in the event of a failure. Additionally, using load balancers can help distribute client connections evenly across the cluster, preventing any one node from becoming overloaded.

Setting up and tuning a Galera Cluster for MariaDB involves configuring the cluster nodes, tuning replication parameters, optimizing storage engine settings, and ensuring network performance is adequate for the replication load. By carefully managing these elements, DBAs can achieve a highly available and scalable MariaDB environment that can handle large-scale workloads with minimal latency. Proper monitoring and proactive management are key to maintaining the reliability and performance of a Galera Cluster over time, ensuring that it can meet the demands of growing applications and datasets.

Using Percona XtraDB Cluster for High Availability

Percona XtraDB Cluster (PXC) is a high-availability solution for MySQL and MariaDB, built on top of the InnoDB storage engine and leveraging Galera Cluster for synchronous multi-master replication. It provides a robust and scalable environment that ensures data consistency, fault tolerance, and automatic failover across multiple nodes. In environments where uptime and data reliability are critical, Percona XtraDB Cluster offers a powerful solution to ensure high availability and minimal downtime. This chapter explores how to set up and use Percona XtraDB Cluster for high availability, discussing the architecture, configuration, and best practices that ensure a stable and efficient deployment.

The core benefit of Percona XtraDB Cluster is its ability to provide synchronous replication. This means that when a write operation is committed on one node, it is immediately replicated across all other nodes in the cluster. This ensures that every node in the cluster is up-to-date and in sync with the others, providing a high level of data consistency. Unlike asynchronous replication, which can result in replication lag and the potential for data inconsistency between master and slave nodes, synchronous replication guarantees that all nodes receive the same updates at the same time. In the case of Percona XtraDB Cluster, the write-set is certified and applied to all nodes in the cluster in a transactionally consistent manner, ensuring that there is no loss of data, even in the event of node failures.

Setting up Percona XtraDB Cluster involves installing Percona Server for MySQL or MariaDB on each node in the cluster and enabling the XtraDB Cluster functionality. The first step in the setup process is to ensure that all nodes in the cluster are running compatible versions of Percona XtraDB Cluster. Once the appropriate versions are installed, the configuration file (my.cnf) on each node must be modified to enable the Galera plugin and set various other configuration parameters that define the cluster behavior. Key parameters to configure include wsrep_on, which enables Galera replication, and wsrep_cluster_address, which specifies the address of the other nodes in the cluster. These parameters allow the nodes to discover each other and form a cluster.

Each node in a Percona XtraDB Cluster must also have a unique wsrep_node_address value, which identifies the node within the cluster. The wsrep_cluster_name parameter ensures that all nodes belong to the same cluster by specifying the cluster's name. It is critical that all nodes in the cluster have the same cluster name to ensure they communicate correctly and function as a cohesive unit. The wsrep_sst_method parameter specifies the state snapshot transfer (SST) method used for bringing new nodes into the cluster, with options such as rsync and xtrabackup being common choices for SST.

Once the cluster is set up and the basic configuration is complete, tuning the Percona XtraDB Cluster for performance is essential. One important consideration is the use of the wsrep_slave_threads parameter, which determines the number of threads available on the node for applying transactions. For systems with high replication traffic, increasing this value can help speed up the application of changes to the slave nodes, thus reducing the time it takes to process replication transactions. However, this value must be set in balance with the system's hardware resources, as setting it too high can lead to contention and reduced performance.

Another key tuning parameter is wsrep_provider_options, which controls various settings related to the internal behavior of the Galera replication protocol. One common option within wsrep_provider_options is flow_control, which helps manage how nodes communicate during high-traffic conditions. By enabling or adjusting the flow_control settings, DBAs can ensure that replication traffic is properly managed, preventing nodes from becoming overwhelmed and potentially falling behind.

In addition to tuning replication parameters, DBAs must also consider other aspects of the cluster's configuration, such as the InnoDB buffer pool size. Percona XtraDB Cluster uses InnoDB as its storage engine, and the performance of InnoDB is heavily influenced by the size of the buffer pool. Ensuring that the buffer pool is large enough to hold a significant portion of the working dataset in memory is critical for reducing disk I/O and improving overall database performance. DBAs should allocate between 60% and 80% of system memory to the InnoDB buffer pool, depending on the size of the dataset and the available system resources.

Another important area for tuning is disk I/O performance. While Percona XtraDB Cluster is designed to handle high levels of concurrency, the speed of the underlying storage subsystem can significantly affect performance. Using solid-state drives (SSDs) for the data directory can drastically reduce I/O latency, especially for write-heavy workloads. Ensuring that the underlying storage system can handle the high write throughput required by the cluster is essential for maintaining replication performance and preventing replication lag.

When using Percona XtraDB Cluster for high availability, one of the most important features is automatic failover. In the event of a node failure, the cluster automatically elects a new node to take over the failed node's role, minimizing downtime and ensuring continued operation. This is particularly useful in environments where uptime is critical and manual intervention is not always possible. However, automatic failover does introduce the need for careful management of node failures. DBAs should ensure that the cluster is properly configured to handle node failures gracefully, preventing data inconsistency or corruption during the failover process. Tools like Orchestrator can help automate failover management by monitoring the cluster's health and automatically promoting a new master when needed.

For high-availability setups, load balancing is also a key consideration. In a typical Percona XtraDB Cluster, all nodes can accept read and write operations. However, directing too many write operations to a single node can cause performance bottlenecks. Using a load balancer can help distribute write operations evenly across the cluster, ensuring that no single node becomes overwhelmed. Similarly, read requests can be distributed to multiple nodes to offload the master node, improving overall read performance. Properly configuring load balancing strategies and ensuring that the load balancer is aware of the cluster's health and node status is essential for maintaining the availability and performance of the cluster.

Monitoring the cluster is also essential for maintaining high availability. Regular monitoring allows DBAs to identify potential issues before they affect the system. Monitoring tools such as Percona Monitoring and Management (PMM), MySQL Enterprise Monitor, or custom scripts can help track key metrics, such as replication lag, node status, and resource utilization. By continuously monitoring these metrics, DBAs can ensure that the cluster is functioning optimally and address any potential problems before they escalate.

Ensuring high availability with Percona XtraDB Cluster requires not only configuring the cluster for optimal performance but also implementing proactive monitoring, load balancing, and failover mechanisms. By tuning various parameters related to replication, storage, and network performance, DBAs can ensure that the cluster performs efficiently and remains reliable under heavy loads. Additionally, using tools like Orchestrator for failover management and PMM for monitoring can help automate tasks and ensure that the cluster continues to function smoothly in the event of node failures or increased traffic. When properly configured, Percona XtraDB Cluster provides a powerful, scalable solution for high-availability MariaDB environments.

Troubleshooting Common Performance Issues in MySQL and MariaDB

MySQL and MariaDB are widely used database management systems, known for their reliability, scalability, and performance. However, even the most robust systems can face performance issues, especially as databases grow in size and complexity. Troubleshooting these performance issues can be a daunting task for database administrators (DBAs), as there are a multitude of factors that can contribute to slow queries, high resource usage, or poor database performance. Identifying the root causes and implementing effective solutions requires a structured approach and a solid understanding of how MySQL and MariaDB operate. This chapter explores some of the most common performance issues in MySQL and MariaDB and provides guidance on how to troubleshoot and resolve them.

One of the most common performance issues in MySQL and MariaDB is slow query performance. Slow queries can significantly degrade the overall performance of a database, especially when they involve complex joins, large datasets, or inefficient indexing. The first step in troubleshooting slow queries is to enable the slow query log, which logs queries that take longer than a specified threshold to execute. By analyzing the slow query log, DBAs can identify which queries are taking the most time and examine their execution plans to determine what may be causing the delays. A common cause of slow queries is the lack of proper indexing. When a query needs to scan an entire table to find the relevant rows, it can be slow, especially if the table is large. By creating appropriate indexes on the columns used in WHERE clauses, JOIN conditions, or ORDER BY clauses, DBAs can significantly improve query performance by reducing the amount of data that needs to be scanned.

Another factor that can cause slow query performance is suboptimal query design. Queries that involve unnecessary joins, subqueries, or complex filtering conditions can be slow, especially when working with large tables. In some cases, rewriting the query to simplify the logic or break it into smaller parts can improve performance. For example, replacing a subquery with a join or using EXISTS instead of IN can sometimes lead to better performance. The EXPLAIN statement is an invaluable tool for analyzing query execution plans. It provides detailed information about how MySQL or MariaDB plans to execute a query, including which indexes will be used and the estimated number of rows to be scanned. By examining the EXPLAIN output, DBAs can identify inefficient operations, such as full table scans or unnecessary joins, and optimize the query accordingly.

In addition to indexing and query optimization, hardware and system resource limitations can also contribute to slow query performance. If the database server is running low on CPU, memory, or disk I/O resources, query execution times can increase. One way to identify resource bottlenecks is by monitoring system performance using tools like top, iostat, or vmstat. If the server is under heavy load, upgrading the hardware or optimizing the system configuration may be necessary. For example, increasing the amount of RAM allocated to the InnoDB buffer pool can improve performance by allowing more data to be cached in memory, reducing the need for disk I/O. Similarly, ensuring that the disk subsystem is fast enough to handle the workload, such as using solid-state drives (SSDs) instead of traditional hard disk drives (HDDs), can help reduce query response times.

Another common performance issue in MySQL and MariaDB is high disk I/O. Excessive disk I/O can lead to slow query performance, as it takes longer for the database to read and write data to disk. InnoDB, the default storage engine for MySQL and MariaDB, uses a buffer pool to cache data and indexes in memory, reducing the need for disk I/O. If the buffer pool is too small, the database will frequently need to access disk, leading to increased latency and slower query performance. DBAs can optimize disk I/O performance by adjusting the innodb_buffer_pool_size parameter to allocate more memory to the buffer pool. Ideally, the buffer pool size should be large enough to hold the working set of data in memory, allowing the database to minimize disk I/O. However, it is important to balance memory allocation to avoid overcommitting system resources.

In addition to the buffer pool, other InnoDB parameters, such as innodb_log_file_size and innodb_io_capacity, can also influence disk I/O performance. The innodb_log_file_size parameter controls the size of the InnoDB redo log files, and increasing this value can reduce the frequency of log file flushes, improving write performance. The innodb_io_capacity parameter determines the number of I/O operations InnoDB will perform per second. Tuning this parameter to match the performance characteristics of the storage system can help optimize disk I/O and prevent bottlenecks.

Another area of concern in MySQL and MariaDB performance is locking and concurrency. In a multi-user environment, multiple transactions may attempt to access the same data simultaneously, leading to contention for locks. MySQL and MariaDB use various locking mechanisms to ensure data consistency, but excessive locking can lead to performance degradation. InnoDB uses row-level locking, which allows multiple transactions to modify different rows in the same table simultaneously. However, if two transactions attempt to modify the same row, a lock conflict will occur, causing one of the transactions to wait for the lock to be released. In some cases, deadlocks can occur, where two or more transactions are waiting for each other to release locks, resulting in a standstill.

To minimize locking issues, DBAs should ensure that transactions are as short as possible. Long-running transactions that hold locks for extended periods can cause contention and lead to performance degradation. By committing or rolling back transactions quickly, DBAs can reduce the time that locks are held and allow other transactions to proceed. Additionally, using appropriate isolation levels can help control the behavior of locks. Lower isolation levels, such as READ COMMITTED, reduce the likelihood of lock conflicts, but they may introduce other issues, such as non-repeatable reads. DBAs must balance the need for data consistency with the potential impact on performance when configuring isolation levels.

Replication latency is another common performance issue in MySQL and MariaDB. In replication setups, where data is copied from the master to one or more slave servers, replication lag can occur if the slave server falls behind the master in processing changes. This can lead to inconsistent data across servers and slow down read queries on the slave. Replication lag can be caused by a variety of factors, including high write volume on the master, slow I/O on the slave, or network latency between the master and slave. To minimize replication lag, DBAs can optimize the master server by ensuring that write operations are fast and efficient. On the slave side, increasing the resources available, such as CPU, memory, and disk I/O, can help the slave catch up with the master more quickly. Monitoring replication status using tools like SHOW SLAVE STATUS can help identify and address lag issues before they become critical.

Finally, MySQL and MariaDB performance can be affected by inefficient database schema design. Poorly designed schemas with excessive joins, non-normalized tables, or missing indexes can cause queries to perform poorly, even on otherwise optimized systems. DBAs should carefully design their schema to minimize redundancy and ensure that data is properly indexed. In particular, indexing frequently queried columns and using composite indexes when appropriate can significantly speed up query execution. Additionally, regularly reviewing and optimizing the schema as the database grows can help maintain performance over time.

Troubleshooting performance issues in MySQL and MariaDB requires a systematic approach that involves identifying bottlenecks, analyzing query execution plans, optimizing system resources, and ensuring that the database schema is designed for efficiency. By monitoring key metrics, adjusting configuration parameters, and optimizing queries and indexing, DBAs can address common performance problems and ensure that their MySQL or MariaDB systems run efficiently and reliably. Regular maintenance, such as optimizing tables and rebuilding indexes, can also help keep the system performing well as the database grows.

Advanced Backup Strategies for High Availability

In the context of high availability, ensuring that data is consistently backed up and can be quickly restored in case of failure is essential. Database backups are a crucial aspect of disaster recovery planning, and while traditional backup strategies are often sufficient for small-scale systems, they may not meet the needs of large, high-traffic, or mission-critical applications. As databases scale, traditional backup methods, such as full backups, can become inefficient and insufficient for ensuring minimal downtime or data loss. Advanced backup strategies that focus on high availability are critical for maintaining business continuity and minimizing the risk of data loss in large-scale environments.

One of the most important considerations in advanced backup strategies for high availability is minimizing downtime during backup operations. Traditional full backups, which copy the entire database, can be time-consuming and resource-intensive, leading to performance degradation during the backup process. This is especially problematic for large databases that experience heavy read and write traffic. To mitigate this, incremental backups or differential backups can be used. These types of backups focus on capturing only the changes made since the last backup, significantly reducing the backup window and the load on the system. By performing frequent incremental backups, DBAs can ensure that backups remain up to date with minimal impact on system performance. Incremental backups can be combined with periodic full backups to maintain a comprehensive backup strategy that ensures both efficiency and data integrity.

For systems with high availability requirements, another important consideration is the ability to perform backups without affecting the production environment. One approach to this is using backup tools that can perform hot backups, which allow backups to be taken while the database is running and accepting queries. In MySQL and MariaDB, tools like Percona XtraBackup provide the ability to perform hot backups for InnoDB databases without locking tables or interrupting normal operations. Hot backups are essential for minimizing downtime and ensuring that the database remains available even during the backup process. Percona XtraBackup, for instance, works by copying the InnoDB data files while the database is still running, ensuring that the backup is consistent and can be restored without requiring downtime. This is particularly useful in high-availability environments where the need for continuous uptime is paramount.

In addition to minimizing downtime during backups, ensuring data consistency across multiple nodes in a distributed database environment is another critical aspect of high-availability backup strategies. In environments using replication, Galera Cluster, or other forms of multi-node database setups, it is important to ensure that all nodes in the system are included in the backup and that the data is consistent across them. A common challenge in multi-node systems is ensuring that the backup captures data in a way that avoids inconsistencies between nodes. To address this, DBAs can employ backup strategies that involve coordinated backups across all nodes, ensuring that the data is consistent and the backup is recoverable on any node in the system. This is particularly important in synchronous replication setups, where data is immediately written to all nodes, as the backup must capture this synchronized state to avoid issues during recovery.

One strategy for consistent multi-node backups is to use point-in-time backups in combination with binary logs. Point-in-time backups capture the state of the database at a specific moment, and using binary logs allows for the recovery of changes that occurred after the backup was taken. By enabling binary logging on the master node and ensuring that all transactions are logged, DBAs can take a point-in-time snapshot of the database and then apply the binary logs to bring the database back to the exact state it was in at the time of the failure. This is particularly useful for recovering from crashes or failures that occur after the backup is taken. Point-in-time recovery ensures that the database can be restored with minimal data loss, and combining this with incremental backups provides an efficient and reliable backup strategy.

To further enhance high-availability backup strategies, offsite backups should be considered. Storing backups locally can be risky if the entire data center goes down due to power failure, fire, or natural disaster.

Offsite backups, either through cloud storage solutions or remote data centers, provide an additional layer of protection by ensuring that backups are stored in separate physical locations. Many organizations use a combination of local and remote backups to ensure data is protected against both hardware failures and catastrophic events. Cloud-based storage solutions offer flexibility and scalability, allowing backups to be stored securely and easily accessed from anywhere. Additionally, cloud providers often offer built-in redundancy and data replication, further ensuring the safety of backups in the event of a failure.

Automating the backup process is another key component of a robust high-availability backup strategy. Manual backups are time-consuming and prone to human error, which can lead to missed backups or inconsistent data. By automating the backup process, DBAs can ensure that backups are performed consistently and on schedule. Automation tools allow backups to be scheduled at regular intervals, such as nightly or weekly, and can be integrated with monitoring systems to alert administrators of any issues during the backup process. Furthermore, automated backup systems can include features such as backup verification, ensuring that backups are successful and that the data can be restored when needed. Verification processes typically involve checking that the backup files are intact, readable, and consistent, as well as performing periodic restore tests to ensure that the backups can be reliably restored.

A critical aspect of backup management in high-availability environments is the ability to quickly restore data when needed. Disaster recovery plans should be in place that outline the steps for restoring the database in case of failure. Backup testing is an essential part of this process. Regularly testing backups ensures that they are valid and can be restored in the event of a failure. DBAs should perform restore drills periodically to test the recovery time objective (RTO) and recovery point objective (RPO), which define how quickly data can be restored and how much data can be lost during a failure. By testing backups and ensuring that the restore process is efficient and reliable, DBAs can ensure that the backup strategy supports the overall high-availability goals of the organization.

For highly transactional systems or environments where data changes rapidly, snapshot-based backups can provide an additional layer of protection. Snapshots allow DBAs to take a point-in-time copy of the database at the storage level, without interrupting the database's operation. Snapshot-based backups are typically faster than traditional backups, and because they capture the entire database state, they are highly useful for ensuring consistency in environments with high transaction rates. However, snapshot backups must be carefully managed to avoid issues such as disk space constraints or incomplete backups if the snapshot is taken during heavy write activity.

Advanced backup strategies for high availability involve careful planning and the use of various tools and techniques to ensure that backups are efficient, consistent, and recoverable. By utilizing hot backups, point-in-time recovery, multi-node coordination, offsite storage, automation, and snapshot technologies, DBAs can create a robust backup strategy that ensures data availability even in the face of system failures. Monitoring and testing backups regularly ensures that the database remains protected and that the recovery process is reliable and efficient, allowing organizations to maintain high availability with minimal data loss.

Restoring Data and Managing Point-in-Time Recovery

Data restoration and point-in-time recovery (PITR) are essential components of database management, especially for systems that require high availability and minimal data loss. Restoring data ensures that a database can be recovered in case of failure, corruption, or other unforeseen events. Point-in-time recovery allows database administrators (DBAs) to restore the database to a specific moment in time, minimizing data loss and ensuring that business operations continue smoothly. Both processes are critical in maintaining data integrity and minimizing downtime, and they require careful planning, strategy, and understanding of the tools available in MySQL and MariaDB.

The process of restoring data typically begins with the selection of the appropriate backup. Backups can vary in type, including full backups, incremental backups, and differential backups, each providing different levels of data protection and recovery options. Full backups capture the entire database at a specific point in time, while incremental and differential backups capture only the changes since the last backup. When restoring data, it is crucial to choose the most recent full backup and combine it with any incremental or differential backups that have been taken in the interim. This allows DBAs to restore the database to the most up-to-date state possible, while minimizing the time required to restore the data.

For MySQL and MariaDB, a popular tool for performing backups and restores is Percona XtraBackup. This tool allows for hot backups, meaning backups can be taken while the database is still running, minimizing downtime during the backup process. Percona XtraBackup can perform both full and incremental backups, and it ensures that the backup is consistent and transactionally safe. To restore data using Percona XtraBackup, DBAs typically restore the full backup first, followed by any incremental backups taken since the full backup was created. The tool allows for seamless integration with MySQL and MariaDB, making it an ideal choice for large, high-traffic systems.

In addition to tools like Percona XtraBackup, MySQL and MariaDB also support the use of binary logs for point-in-time recovery. Binary logs contain a record of all changes made to the database, including insertions, updates, and deletions. By enabling binary logging, DBAs can ensure that every change to the database is recorded and available for recovery. When performing a point-in-time recovery, the DBAs restore the most recent full backup and then apply the binary logs that were generated after the backup was taken. This allows the database to be restored to a specific moment in time, minimizing data loss between the last backup and the point of recovery.

Point-in-time recovery is particularly useful in situations where data corruption or accidental data loss occurs. For example, if a user accidentally deletes critical data or if a transaction is mistakenly rolled back, the ability to restore the database to the exact point before the incident occurred can prevent significant data loss. The PITR process allows the DBA to roll forward from the last valid backup using the binary logs, effectively undoing the unwanted changes and restoring the database to its previous state.

To effectively manage point-in-time recovery, it is important to ensure that binary logging is enabled and properly configured in MySQL or MariaDB. The log_bin parameter in the configuration file controls whether binary logging is enabled, and the log_bin_basename parameter specifies the base name for the binary log files. The binlog_format parameter determines the format of the binary logs, with options including STATEMENT, ROW, and MIXED formats. The ROW format, which logs changes at the row level, is often the most reliable for point-in-time recovery, as it ensures that every change is recorded precisely, even when updates affect multiple rows in a single table.

It is also essential to configure the expire_logs_days parameter, which specifies how long binary logs are retained before being automatically deleted. This is crucial for managing disk space and ensuring that old logs do not accumulate unnecessarily. However, this retention period must be balanced with the need for recovery, as older binary logs may be required for restoring the database to a specific point in time. DBAs should regularly monitor the availability of binary logs and ensure that they are properly archived for disaster recovery purposes.

One important consideration when using point-in-time recovery is the risk of applying binary logs in the wrong order. Inconsistent application of binary logs can lead to data corruption or other issues. To avoid this, DBAs should carefully track the binary log positions and timestamps. Each entry in the binary log includes a position value, which can be used to determine where the log entries should be applied. By carefully managing the positions and applying the logs in the correct sequence, DBAs can ensure that the recovery process is both accurate and reliable.

Another factor to consider when performing point-in-time recovery is the impact on replication in master-slave setups. In a replication environment, applying binary logs to the master can affect the consistency of the replica servers. After performing a point-in-time recovery on the master, the binary logs need to be synchronized with the slave servers to ensure that they are also restored to the same state.

In many cases, it is necessary to stop replication temporarily while the master is restored, and then resume replication once the master and slave are in sync. This process ensures that the replication setup remains consistent and that no data is lost during the recovery.

DBAs should also be aware of the recovery time objective (RTO) and recovery point objective (RPO) when implementing backup and recovery strategies. The RTO refers to the maximum allowable downtime during a disaster recovery scenario, while the RPO defines the maximum amount of data loss that can be tolerated. By performing regular backup and restore drills, DBAs can ensure that recovery processes meet the desired RTO and RPO. These drills should include point-in-time recovery tests to ensure that the process works smoothly and that the DBA is familiar with the steps involved.

In addition to binary logs, another method of point-in-time recovery in MySQL and MariaDB is the use of snapshots. Snapshots capture the state of the database at a specific moment in time and can be used to restore the database to that point. Snapshot-based backups can be faster than traditional backup methods, especially in environments with large datasets. However, it is important to note that snapshots should be taken on consistent storage, and the database should be in a consistent state when the snapshot is captured to avoid corruption during recovery.

Database administrators must carefully consider their organization's specific recovery requirements and implement a backup and recovery strategy that meets both performance and reliability needs. Effective management of data restoration and point-in-time recovery not only ensures that databases can be quickly restored after failure but also provides confidence in the system's resilience. By enabling binary logging, implementing regular full and incremental backups, and performing periodic recovery drills, DBAs can ensure that their MySQL or MariaDB systems are prepared to recover with minimal data loss and downtime in the event of a failure.

Monitoring MySQL and MariaDB Performance with Metrics

Monitoring the performance of MySQL and MariaDB is crucial for ensuring that the databases run efficiently, handle workloads effectively, and avoid downtime. As databases grow in size and complexity, tracking performance becomes essential for identifying bottlenecks, preventing resource exhaustion, and maintaining system health. Effective monitoring involves collecting a wide range of performance metrics that provide insights into the database's behavior. These metrics help database administrators (DBAs) understand how well the system is performing, identify potential issues, and make data-driven decisions to optimize the database environment. This chapter explores how to monitor MySQL and MariaDB performance using key metrics, what these metrics reveal, and how they can be used to enhance overall database performance.

The first step in monitoring MySQL and MariaDB performance is understanding the most important metrics that provide insight into the health of the database. Key performance indicators (KPIs) include metrics related to server performance, query execution, memory usage, disk I/O, and replication. Monitoring these metrics allows DBAs to detect slow queries, track resource consumption, and identify any potential system failures before they impact performance.

One of the most essential areas to monitor is server resource utilization. Metrics related to CPU usage, memory consumption, and disk I/O are critical for understanding how well the system is handling its workload. High CPU usage can indicate that queries or processes are consuming more processing power than necessary. If CPU usage consistently remains high, it could mean that queries are inefficient or that the server needs more CPU resources to handle the load. Similarly, monitoring memory usage provides valuable insight into whether the database is operating within its allocated memory limits. If the system starts swapping to disk due to insufficient RAM, it can lead to significant performance degradation. Monitoring tools like top, htop, or the SHOW STATUS command can provide real-time data on system performance, including memory usage and CPU load.

Disk I/O is another critical metric that can impact MySQL and MariaDB performance. A high rate of disk reads and writes can be indicative of an underlying performance bottleneck. Database operations, especially on large datasets, require significant disk I/O, and if the storage system is not optimized, it can slow down query execution. Monitoring disk activity can help DBAs identify excessive disk I/O, which may be caused by inefficient queries, inadequate storage, or insufficient indexing. Disk I/O metrics, such as Innodb_buffer_pool_reads, Innodb_buffer_pool_write_requests, and Innodb_io_capacity, provide valuable insights into the efficiency of the database's storage system.

Another important aspect of database performance monitoring is query performance. The efficiency of queries directly impacts overall database performance, and identifying slow queries is crucial for maintaining high throughput. MySQL and MariaDB offer tools for tracking slow queries, such as the slow query log. Enabling the slow query log allows DBAs to capture queries that take longer than a specified threshold to execute. Analyzing these queries can reveal patterns that point to inefficiencies, such as missing indexes, suboptimal query structure, or large table scans. The EXPLAIN command is a valuable tool for analyzing query execution plans. It shows how MySQL or MariaDB plans to execute a query, including which indexes are being used and how many rows will be scanned. By using EXPLAIN, DBAs can identify problematic queries and optimize them for better performance.

Index usage is another key factor in query performance. When queries do not leverage indexes efficiently, they can result in full table scans that put unnecessary strain on the database. Monitoring index usage metrics, such as Handler_read_rnd_next, Handler_read_key, and Handler_insert, can provide insights into how often indexes are used and whether certain queries are causing unnecessary full table scans. By ensuring that the most frequently queried columns are indexed, DBAs can reduce the number of rows that need to be scanned, improving query execution times.

In addition to query performance, it is essential to monitor the efficiency of the InnoDB storage engine, which is the default for MySQL and MariaDB. InnoDB uses a buffer pool to cache data and indexes in memory, reducing the need for disk I/O. Monitoring the Innodb_buffer_pool_size, Innodb_buffer_pool_reads, and Innodb_buffer_pool_write_requests metrics provides valuable insights into the effectiveness of the buffer pool. If the buffer pool is too small, the database will need to perform more disk I/O, leading to slower query execution. By increasing the buffer pool size to fit the working dataset, DBAs can reduce the need for disk access and improve performance. Additionally, monitoring the Innodb_log_file_size and Innodb_log_buffer_size metrics is essential for ensuring that InnoDB's transaction logs are configured optimally, as inefficient log file sizes can lead to slow write operations.

Replication is another area that requires monitoring, especially in environments with master-slave or multi-master replication. Replication lag can occur when there is a delay in copying changes from the master to the slave, leading to data inconsistency. Monitoring replication lag metrics such as Seconds_Behind_Master can help DBAs identify if replication is falling behind and determine the cause. Common causes of replication lag include slow queries on the master, inadequate resources on the slave, or network latency between nodes. To mitigate replication lag, DBAs can optimize query performance, ensure that the slave is properly sized to handle the replication load, and address network issues that may contribute to delays.

For high-availability environments, where uptime is critical, monitoring failover and node health is essential. Percona Monitoring and Management (PMM) or other third-party monitoring tools can provide comprehensive monitoring for MySQL and MariaDB, including replication status, server health, and performance metrics. These tools allow DBAs to set up alerts based on predefined thresholds for key performance metrics, enabling proactive management of the database environment. For example, if replication lag exceeds a certain threshold, the DBA can be alerted before it affects application performance. Similarly, monitoring tools can track the status of nodes in a clustered environment, ensuring that all nodes are operating properly and that failover mechanisms are working as expected.

Data consistency is also a critical aspect of performance monitoring in MySQL and MariaDB. In high-availability setups, it is essential to ensure that data is consistent across all nodes. Monitoring the consistency of the buffer pool and replication logs can help detect discrepancies that might affect performance. For example, if nodes in a Galera cluster or multi-master setup are not in sync, it could lead to inconsistencies in the data, which might result in slow queries or application errors. Monitoring tools can alert DBAs if data inconsistency is detected, allowing them to take corrective actions before performance issues arise.

To ensure optimal performance, DBAs must also monitor the system's configuration parameters and adjust them as necessary based on the observed metrics. Regular performance audits and configuration reviews help ensure that MySQL and MariaDB are tuned to handle the workload efficiently. By continually monitoring key metrics, DBAs can identify emerging performance issues, prevent potential bottlenecks, and optimize system resources to ensure that the database remains responsive and reliable under heavy loads.

In summary, monitoring MySQL and MariaDB performance through a comprehensive set of metrics is essential for maintaining the health of the database system. By keeping track of server resource utilization, query performance, disk I/O, replication health, and system configurations, DBAs can identify potential issues early, optimize queries, and ensure high availability. Effective monitoring provides the insights needed to keep MySQL and MariaDB environments running efficiently and ensures that the databases continue to meet the performance demands of modern applications.

Using Performance Schema to Diagnose Slow Queries

MySQL and MariaDB are widely used database management systems, providing efficient and scalable solutions for managing large amounts of data. However, as with any database system, performance issues can arise, particularly with complex queries or high-traffic environments. Diagnosing slow queries and identifying their root causes is critical for optimizing database performance and ensuring that systems continue to run smoothly. One of the most powerful tools available to database administrators (DBAs) for diagnosing slow queries is the Performance Schema, a feature built into MySQL and MariaDB that collects and organizes detailed performance data about query execution. By utilizing the Performance Schema, DBAs can gain deep insights into query behavior, identify bottlenecks, and take corrective action to optimize query performance.

The Performance Schema is a monitoring tool that tracks various performance metrics at the server, session, and statement levels. It provides a wealth of data, including detailed information about query execution times, resource consumption, and potential inefficiencies. One of the most significant advantages of the Performance Schema is that it can capture performance data with minimal overhead, allowing DBAs to diagnose slow queries in production environments without significantly impacting database performance. To enable the Performance Schema, the database must be configured with specific settings in the my.cnf configuration file. In most cases, the Performance Schema is enabled by default in recent versions of MySQL and MariaDB, but DBAs may need to ensure that the appropriate tables are created and the necessary settings are configured to capture the desired data.

Once the Performance Schema is enabled, it begins collecting data on various aspects of query execution, including the execution time, wait events, and the resources used by individual queries. This information is stored in a series of tables within the Performance Schema, such as events_statements_summary_by_digest, events_statements_history, and events_waits_summary_by_instance. These tables can be queried to analyze slow queries and identify patterns that may indicate performance issues. For example, by querying the events_statements_summary_by_digest table, DBAs can identify queries that take the longest time to execute, how often they are executed, and the average time spent on each execution. This allows DBAs to prioritize optimization efforts by focusing on the queries that have the greatest impact on overall performance.

In addition to identifying slow queries, the Performance Schema provides detailed information about the resources consumed by each query. By monitoring metrics such as CPU usage, disk I/O, and memory consumption, DBAs can gain insights into which queries are putting the most strain on system resources. For instance, a query that performs excessive disk I/O may be an indication that it is not using indexes efficiently, leading to unnecessary table scans. Similarly, high CPU usage could suggest that the query involves complex calculations or joins that could be optimized. By understanding the resource usage of slow queries, DBAs can take targeted actions to optimize them, such as adding indexes, rewriting queries, or adjusting server configurations to better handle the load.

Another valuable feature of the Performance Schema is its ability to track wait events, which are events that occur when a query or process is waiting for a resource, such as disk I/O, locks, or network communication. Wait events are a common cause of slow queries, as they introduce delays during query execution. The Performance Schema captures information about these wait events, allowing DBAs to identify which resources are causing the most significant delays. For example, if queries are consistently waiting for I/O, it may indicate that the disk subsystem is not fast enough to handle the volume of queries being executed. If queries are waiting on locks, it may suggest that there is contention between concurrent transactions, possibly due to poorly optimized locking strategies or long-running transactions. By identifying these wait events, DBAs can address the underlying issues, such as optimizing disk I/O, adjusting locking strategies, or tuning other system parameters.

The Performance Schema also tracks the lifetime of a query and its associated events, providing DBAs with insights into how long a query spends in various stages of execution. This information can be useful for identifying where inefficiencies exist within the query execution process. For example, a query may spend a significant amount of time parsing or planning before it is executed, indicating that there are opportunities for optimization in the query structure or indexing. Alternatively, a query may spend too much time in the commit phase, suggesting that the database's transaction management system may need tuning. By breaking down the execution process into these phases, the Performance Schema helps DBAs pinpoint where delays are occurring and take action to address them.

In addition to using the Performance Schema for diagnosing slow queries, DBAs can use it to monitor long-running transactions and deadlocks. The Performance Schema captures detailed information about the duration of transactions, as well as any potential deadlocks that may occur. By monitoring the status of transactions, DBAs can identify transactions that are holding locks for extended periods and causing contention with other queries. In high-traffic systems, long-running transactions can significantly impact overall performance, so identifying and addressing these transactions is essential for maintaining smooth database operation. Similarly, deadlocks, which occur when two or more transactions are waiting for each other to release locks, can lead to transaction failures and poor performance. The Performance Schema provides information on deadlock events, allowing DBAs to identify the causes and take corrective action, such as adjusting the transaction isolation level or optimizing the queries involved.

Using the Performance Schema requires a strategic approach, as the amount of data it collects can be extensive, particularly in busy environments with high query throughput. To avoid overwhelming the system with excessive data collection, DBAs can fine-tune the Performance Schema configuration to focus on specific metrics that are most relevant to their performance diagnosis. For example, DBAs can limit the capture of events to specific query types or set thresholds for recording data only when certain criteria are met, such as when a query exceeds a certain execution time. This allows for more efficient use of resources while still capturing the necessary data to identify slow queries and performance bottlenecks.

Integrating the Performance Schema with other monitoring tools can enhance its effectiveness. For instance, tools like Percona Monitoring and Management (PMM) or MySQL Enterprise Monitor can provide a graphical interface for visualizing Performance Schema data, making it easier for DBAs to identify performance trends and issues. These tools can also provide alerts when certain thresholds are exceeded, helping DBAs proactively manage database performance before issues escalate.

In environments with complex query workloads or high-traffic applications, the Performance Schema is a powerful tool for identifying and addressing slow queries. By analyzing the data collected by the Performance Schema, DBAs can gain deep insights into query execution, resource usage, and wait events, enabling them to optimize performance effectively. Whether it is identifying missing indexes, addressing query inefficiencies, or resolving lock contention, the Performance Schema provides the detailed, actionable data needed to keep MySQL and MariaDB systems running at peak performance. By leveraging the full capabilities of the Performance Schema, DBAs can ensure that their databases remain responsive, efficient, and capable of handling increasing workloads.

Using MySQL Enterprise Monitor for Proactive Monitoring

MySQL Enterprise Monitor is a comprehensive monitoring tool designed to help database administrators (DBAs) maintain the health and performance of their MySQL and MariaDB environments. As databases grow in size and complexity, it becomes increasingly difficult to manually monitor every aspect of the system, and that's where MySQL Enterprise Monitor comes into play. It offers an integrated solution for proactive monitoring, providing real-time insights into server performance, query execution, system resource utilization, and potential issues that could lead to downtime or degraded performance. By utilizing MySQL Enterprise Monitor, DBAs can quickly identify and resolve problems, ensuring that the database remains available, secure, and performant under heavy load.

The core functionality of MySQL Enterprise Monitor revolves around providing real-time data and insights into the health of MySQL and MariaDB instances. It helps DBAs monitor key performance metrics, such as CPU usage, memory consumption, disk I/O, and network activity, which are critical for understanding how the database is performing. These metrics allow DBAs to assess the overall system health, identify potential bottlenecks, and prevent issues before they affect the application. The monitor collects data at both the server level and the query level, providing a holistic view of the system and enabling DBAs to troubleshoot issues that may arise from both resource limitations and inefficient queries.

One of the key features of MySQL Enterprise Monitor is its ability to monitor query performance in real time. It tracks slow queries, resource consumption, and execution times, which helps DBAs identify queries that may be consuming excessive resources or taking longer than expected. By capturing detailed information on query performance, such as query execution plans and query duration, DBAs can optimize slow or resource-heavy queries, improving the overall efficiency of the database. The tool also provides historical query performance data, which can be useful for identifying trends over time and pinpointing areas where optimization is needed. Through this continuous monitoring, MySQL Enterprise Monitor enables proactive management of query performance, preventing issues before they impact end users.

In addition to query performance, MySQL Enterprise Monitor helps DBAs monitor the health of the MySQL or MariaDB server itself. It tracks the performance of key system components, such as the InnoDB storage engine, replication status, and various database metrics like buffer pool size, transaction rates, and connection counts. With this data, DBAs can quickly detect issues such as high CPU utilization, memory bottlenecks, or disk I/O problems that may be affecting the database's ability to handle requests efficiently. Furthermore, MySQL Enterprise Monitor provides alerts for predefined thresholds, enabling DBAs to receive immediate notifications when a problem arises, such as when a server is running low on disk space or when query performance starts to degrade.

MySQL Enterprise Monitor also supports monitoring of replication environments, making it particularly useful in high-availability setups. Replication health is a critical aspect of high-availability systems, and any lag or failure in replication can lead to data inconsistency or downtime. MySQL Enterprise Monitor tracks replication status and provides real-time information on replication lag, ensuring that DBAs are immediately alerted if the slave servers fall behind the master. Additionally, the monitor offers detailed insights into replication performance, such as the number of transactions being replicated and the replication delay, helping DBAs resolve issues before they affect the system's availability. With its proactive monitoring capabilities, MySQL Enterprise Monitor ensures that replication environments are running smoothly and that failover mechanisms can be triggered quickly in the event of a failure.

Another significant advantage of MySQL Enterprise Monitor is its ability to track server configurations and ensure that they are optimized for performance. The monitor provides detailed information about the server's configuration settings, comparing them against best practices and recommending adjustments where necessary. For example, it can identify settings related to memory allocation, query cache size, and other server parameters that may be suboptimal for the workload. By providing actionable recommendations, MySQL Enterprise Monitor helps DBAs optimize the server's configuration for better performance and stability, reducing the likelihood of system slowdowns or crashes due to misconfiguration.

MySQL Enterprise Monitor also provides a centralized view of all monitored MySQL and MariaDB instances, making it easy for DBAs to manage large and complex database environments. The monitor's web-based interface allows DBAs to access performance data, receive alerts, and manage server configurations from a single dashboard. This centralized view simplifies the management of multiple database instances, enabling DBAs to track the health and performance of each server, whether it is a standalone instance, part of a replication setup, or part of a clustered environment. The monitor also supports the management of various MySQL and MariaDB versions, providing flexibility in multi-version environments.

In terms of scalability, MySQL Enterprise Monitor is well-suited for large environments with many database instances. It can handle multiple servers across different geographical locations, providing DBAs with a unified monitoring solution that scales as the database infrastructure grows. The tool allows DBAs to organize their servers into groups, making it easier to manage and monitor large numbers of servers, and providing a more efficient way to handle notifications and alerts for different sets of instances. This makes MySQL Enterprise Monitor a valuable tool for organizations that need to maintain high availability and performance across multiple database environments.

The ability to automate tasks and optimize workflows is another key feature of MySQL Enterprise Monitor. By providing a set of APIs and integration options, the monitor enables DBAs to automate common database management tasks, such as backup scheduling, log analysis, and server configuration changes. This can help streamline database administration, reduce the risk of human error, and ensure that database systems remain well-maintained. The monitor's automation capabilities are particularly useful for organizations with large, complex database environments that require frequent updates and maintenance tasks.

Furthermore, MySQL Enterprise Monitor provides security-related metrics, helping DBAs ensure that the database is configured securely and protected from unauthorized access. The tool tracks user activity, login attempts, and access controls, providing valuable insights into potential security risks. It can also alert DBAs if there are security-related anomalies, such as excessive failed login attempts or unauthorized privilege changes, allowing them to respond promptly and mitigate potential security threats.

By integrating MySQL Enterprise Monitor into daily database operations, DBAs gain a powerful tool that helps them maintain the health, availability, and performance of their MySQL and MariaDB environments. Its real-time monitoring, alerting, and detailed performance insights ensure that DBAs can proactively address issues before they escalate, ensuring that the database performs optimally and remains available. As database environments continue to grow in size and complexity, MySQL Enterprise Monitor provides the necessary visibility and tools to manage performance effectively, ensuring the reliability and scalability of MySQL and MariaDB databases in production environments.

Managing and Tuning Temporary Tables in MySQL and MariaDB

Temporary tables are a powerful feature in MySQL and MariaDB that provide a mechanism for storing intermediate results during query execution. These tables allow for efficient handling of complex queries, where intermediate data must be processed or manipulated before producing the final result. However, while temporary tables can significantly improve query performance, improper management or tuning can lead to performance bottlenecks, excessive disk usage, and other inefficiencies. Understanding how to manage and tune temporary tables is critical for ensuring that MySQL and MariaDB systems perform optimally under varying workloads.

Temporary tables are automatically created by MySQL or MariaDB when a query requires intermediate data storage. For example, when performing complex joins, aggregations, or subqueries, the database engine may create a temporary table to store intermediate results before returning the final output. These temporary tables are typically session-specific, meaning that they exist only for the duration of the session or until the connection is closed. When a query is executed, MySQL or MariaDB decides whether to store the temporary table in memory or on disk, depending on its size and the configuration settings. The ability to use memory for temporary tables provides a significant performance advantage, as memory-based tables are much faster than disk-based ones.

By default, temporary tables are stored in memory, using the MEMORY storage engine. This is advantageous because memory access is significantly faster than disk access, leading to reduced query execution times. However, memory is a finite resource, and when temporary tables become too large to fit in memory, they are written to disk using the InnoDB or the MyISAM storage engines. Disk-based temporary tables are slower to read and write compared to in-memory tables, which can result in a noticeable performance degradation. This transition from memory to disk can occur when a temporary table exceeds the size of the tmp_table_size or max_heap_table_size parameters. If these parameters are not appropriately configured, queries that require large temporary tables can suffer from significant performance bottlenecks.

The tmp_table_size and max_heap_table_size parameters control the maximum size of in-memory temporary tables. These two settings are crucial for determining when MySQL or MariaDB will switch from memory-based temporary tables to disk-based ones. By increasing these parameters, DBAs can ensure that larger temporary tables are stored in memory, improving query performance. However, increasing these values also means allocating more memory, which could impact the performance of other processes running on the server. It is essential to find a balance between providing enough memory for temporary tables and leaving sufficient resources for other database operations.

In addition to the tmp_table_size and max_heap_table_size parameters, there are other settings that influence the handling of temporary tables. The tmpdir parameter specifies the directory where disk-based temporary tables are stored. By default, this directory is set to the system's temporary directory, but it can be changed to a dedicated location with faster storage, such as an SSD. Storing temporary tables on faster storage can significantly reduce the time it takes to read and write disk-based tables, mitigating the performance impact of large temporary tables. It is also a good practice to monitor disk space usage, as excessive disk-based temporary tables can lead to running out of disk space, causing MySQL or MariaDB to fail.

When dealing with large datasets and complex queries, using indexes on temporary tables can also improve performance. Although temporary tables do not require permanent indexing, indexing them appropriately during query execution can speed up the retrieval of data, especially in cases where the temporary table will be used in subsequent queries. The CREATE INDEX statement can be used to add indexes to temporary tables after they are created. However, adding indexes introduces some overhead during table creation and insertion, so it is important to consider the specific use case and query patterns before adding indexes to temporary tables.

Another aspect of managing temporary tables is ensuring that they are properly cleaned up after use. Since temporary tables are automatically dropped at the end of a session or query, it is generally not necessary to manually drop them. However, if a large number of temporary tables are created during complex or long-running queries, it is important to ensure that they do not consume excessive resources. DBAs should be aware of the server's resource usage, including memory and disk space, and check for any lingering temporary tables that may not have been cleaned up properly. Monitoring tools and logs can help identify such issues and ensure that resources are efficiently utilized.

In highly concurrent environments, temporary tables can also introduce contention issues. When multiple queries are executed simultaneously, they may attempt to create or access temporary tables at the same time, leading to locking and resource contention. In these cases, the performance of the database can degrade significantly, especially if temporary tables are large or involve complex operations. To mitigate this, it is crucial to optimize the queries that create and use temporary tables, ensuring that they are as efficient as possible. Additionally, ensuring that the system has sufficient memory and disk I/O resources can help reduce contention and improve overall performance.

One of the key strategies for tuning the performance of temporary tables is query optimization. Complex queries that require the use of temporary tables can often be optimized to reduce the need for large temporary tables. For example, breaking down a large query into smaller parts or using subqueries with more selective conditions can reduce the amount of data that needs to be stored in temporary tables. Similarly, simplifying joins and filtering data before creating temporary tables can reduce the size and complexity of the tables, improving overall performance. By optimizing the underlying queries, DBAs can reduce the burden on temporary tables and improve the performance of the entire database system.

For environments that require frequent creation and usage of temporary tables, such as data warehousing or reporting systems, it may be beneficial to implement a dedicated memory-based storage solution. In these cases, utilizing in-memory databases or dedicated in-memory caches can help speed up query performance and reduce the reliance on disk-based temporary tables. For example, Redis or Memcached can be used in conjunction with MySQL or MariaDB to store intermediate query results, reducing the need to create large temporary tables.

Managing and tuning temporary tables is an essential aspect of ensuring optimal performance in MySQL and MariaDB environments. By configuring the appropriate parameters for in-memory table sizes, utilizing faster storage for disk-based tables, and optimizing queries that use temporary tables, DBAs can significantly improve query performance and minimize resource consumption. Furthermore, by regularly monitoring resource usage and ensuring that temporary tables are properly cleaned up, DBAs can prevent issues related to excessive memory or disk consumption. With careful management and tuning, temporary tables can be a powerful tool for enhancing the efficiency of complex queries while maintaining high performance across the database system.

Tuning the MySQL and MariaDB Connection Pool

Efficient management of database connections is essential for maintaining the performance and stability of MySQL and MariaDB databases, especially in high-traffic environments where many clients simultaneously access the database. The connection pool is a vital aspect of database performance, as it helps reduce the overhead associated with establishing and closing database connections. By reusing a set of pre-established database connections, the connection pool minimizes the time and resources spent on connection creation, which can be particularly costly in terms of CPU usage and network bandwidth. Tuning the connection pool in MySQL and MariaDB is therefore an important task for DBAs, enabling them to optimize the efficiency of their database systems and improve overall throughput.

The connection pool in MySQL and MariaDB is responsible for managing the database connections that are used by client applications. When a client application needs to execute a query, it requests a connection from the pool. If a connection is available, it is allocated to the client; otherwise, the client must wait for a connection to become available. After the query is executed, the connection is returned to the pool for reuse by other clients. The goal of the connection pool is to ensure that the number of connections remains manageable, preventing excessive overhead from repeatedly creating and destroying connections.

One of the first steps in tuning the MySQL and MariaDB connection pool is determining the optimal number of connections that the system can handle. The maximum number of connections is controlled by the max_connections parameter, which defines the upper limit of simultaneous connections allowed to the database. Setting this value too low can cause clients to experience delays when trying to establish a connection, while setting it too high can result in excessive memory usage and potential performance degradation. The optimal value for max_connections depends on the system's resources, such as available memory and CPU, as well as the expected workload and traffic patterns. DBAs should carefully monitor connection usage and adjust this parameter to ensure that the system can handle peak load without overburdening the server.

In addition to max_connections, there are other parameters that control the behavior of the connection pool, including wait_timeout and interactive_timeout. The wait_timeout parameter defines the amount of time a connection can remain idle before it is closed by the server. If a connection is not used within this time frame, the server will automatically terminate it to free up resources. The interactive_timeout parameter works similarly, but it specifically applies to interactive sessions, such as those initiated by a client running the MySQL or MariaDB command-line client. Tuning these timeout values is essential to ensure that connections are closed promptly when they are no longer needed, helping to avoid unnecessary resource consumption. Setting these values too high can lead to a buildup of idle connections, while setting them too low can result in clients being disconnected too frequently, leading to connection overhead.

Another important aspect of connection pool tuning is controlling the number of threads used to handle connections. MySQL and MariaDB use threads to manage incoming client connections, and the number of threads is controlled by the thread_handling parameter. In high-concurrency environments, it may be necessary to adjust this parameter to ensure that the system can handle a large number of connections efficiently. The thread_handling parameter has several possible values, including one-thread-per-connection, which creates a new thread for each connection, and pool-of-threads, which uses a fixed pool of threads to handle multiple connections. The pool-of-threads option can be particularly useful for environments with high connection throughput, as it reduces the overhead associated with creating and destroying threads for each connection.

DBAs should also consider using a connection pool manager, such as the one provided by MySQL or MariaDB's third-party tools, to further optimize connection management. Connection pool managers are designed to efficiently allocate and manage connections from a pool, ensuring that connections are reused as efficiently as possible and that the number of connections remains within the system's capacity. These tools allow for finer-grained control over connection settings, such as maximum connection wait times, connection retries, and connection reuse strategies. By using a connection pool manager, DBAs can reduce the overhead associated with managing database connections and improve the responsiveness of the database system.

Monitoring the connection pool is crucial for identifying potential performance issues related to connection management. MySQL and MariaDB provide various status variables and monitoring tools to track connection pool behavior, including Threads_connected, which indicates the current number of active connections, and Max_used_connections, which shows the highest number of connections used at any given time. By monitoring these values, DBAs can identify trends in connection usage and adjust connection pool parameters accordingly. If the Max_used_connections value is consistently close to the max_connections limit, it may indicate that the system is under heavy load and that the connection pool size needs to be increased. Conversely, if the number of idle connections is consistently high, it may suggest that the wait_timeout value is too large and that connections are not being closed efficiently.

In environments with high availability or load-balanced database clusters, managing the connection pool becomes even more important. Load balancers distribute incoming queries across multiple database instances to ensure even traffic distribution and high availability. In such setups, it is essential that the connection pool is managed across all database nodes, ensuring that connections are properly distributed and that no node is overwhelmed with requests. Connection pooling tools can help balance connections across multiple nodes in the cluster, improving overall performance and reducing the likelihood of connection bottlenecks. Additionally, in multi-master replication setups, ensuring that connections are appropriately distributed across all masters is crucial for maintaining performance and preventing any single node from becoming a bottleneck.

For applications that use persistent database connections, such as web applications, it is important to ensure that the connection pool is configured to handle the peak connection load. Persistent connections can improve performance by reusing existing connections across multiple requests, reducing the overhead associated with connection creation. However, persistent connections can also lead to resource contention if not managed properly. By monitoring connection usage and adjusting connection pool settings, DBAs can ensure that the system handles persistent connections efficiently, preventing excessive resource consumption and ensuring that connections are reused effectively.

Connection pooling is not only about managing the number of connections, but also about optimizing the query execution time for each connection. Connections should be managed in such a way that the database can execute queries as quickly as possible, without unnecessary overhead. For example, if connections are allocated inefficiently or queries are taking longer than expected, the overall system performance can suffer. Proper connection pool tuning allows the system to minimize waiting times and execute queries in a timely manner, even under high load.

Finally, regular audits of connection pool performance should be part of the DBA's routine. As traffic patterns and workloads change over time, connection pool parameters should be reviewed and adjusted accordingly. This ensures that the database system remains responsive and can handle varying loads without degradation in performance. Using tools like MySQL Enterprise Monitor or other third-party monitoring solutions, DBAs can regularly assess the health of the connection pool and identify areas for improvement.

Tuning the MySQL and MariaDB connection pool involves a combination of adjusting server parameters, optimizing thread handling, and using specialized connection pool managers to ensure efficient use of resources. By actively monitoring connection usage, adjusting configuration settings, and ensuring that the connection pool is effectively managing incoming queries, DBAs can maintain optimal performance across their database systems. Proper connection pool management leads to more efficient database operations, ensuring that applications can scale effectively and perform reliably, even under heavy loads.

Security Implications for Performance Tuning

When it comes to performance tuning for MySQL and MariaDB, there is often a focus on optimizing queries, adjusting configuration settings, and enhancing system resources to improve database speed and responsiveness. However, it is equally important to consider the security implications that arise from performance tuning. While making changes to improve performance, it is crucial to ensure that those adjustments do not compromise the security of the database system. The balance between performance optimization and maintaining a secure environment requires careful consideration, as certain tuning decisions may inadvertently expose the system to security vulnerabilities or weaken its defenses.

One of the key areas where security and performance tuning intersect is in the management of user privileges. As performance optimizations are made, such as changing query execution plans, adding indexes, or altering database configurations, the need to control access to the database becomes even more critical. If a DBA focuses solely on performance without considering proper access control mechanisms, it could result in unintended data exposure or unauthorized access. For example, if broad privileges are granted to users in an attempt to ease management or improve efficiency, it may lead to scenarios where unauthorized users can access or modify sensitive data. This would not only be a violation of security best practices but also potentially introduce vulnerabilities. Therefore, maintaining the principle of least privilege should always be a priority, even when tuning the database for better performance.

In addition to user privileges, performance tuning can sometimes involve changes to the way sensitive data is stored or accessed. For example, tuning storage engines or modifying index structures to improve query speed may also impact the encryption or masking of sensitive data. If proper encryption mechanisms are not considered during performance tuning, it can lead to the exposure of sensitive data in unencrypted forms. For instance, altering the way data is indexed or cached could inadvertently bypass encryption policies, especially if sensitive fields are stored without proper encryption. As performance enhancements are made, DBAs must ensure that encryption methods, such as Transparent Data Encryption (TDE) or SSL connections, are not compromised and are consistently applied to sensitive data throughout the database.

Another area where performance tuning can have security implications is in the configuration of database connections and network settings. In a bid to optimize query performance, DBAs may make changes to connection handling, such as increasing the number of allowed connections or adjusting timeouts. While these changes can reduce latency and improve user experience, they may also open up the system to potential denial-of-service (DoS) attacks or brute-force login attempts. For example, increasing the max_connections parameter without proper control over login attempts can lead to an overload of connections, allowing attackers to exhaust available connections and disrupt legitimate access. Similarly, adjusting timeouts for better performance without considering the security risks could leave the system vulnerable to long-running queries or connections that could be exploited for resource exhaustion. Therefore, careful attention must be paid to connection parameters such as max_connections, wait_timeout, and interactive_timeout to balance performance improvements with protection against unauthorized access.

The use of caching mechanisms, such as query caching or application-level caching, is another common performance optimization. While caching can significantly reduce query execution time and improve the user experience, it also introduces a potential security risk if sensitive data is inadvertently cached. For instance, caching user data or session information can lead to the accidental exposure of sensitive information if the cache is not properly secured. Caching sensitive queries or results without proper access control can make it easier for attackers to gain unauthorized access to confidential information. Therefore, when implementing caching solutions for performance optimization, it is essential to ensure that cache data is encrypted and that only authorized users can access cached results. Additionally,

DBAs should be aware of the security risks associated with stale data in caches, ensuring that cache invalidation mechanisms are in place to prevent the use of outdated information.

Database replication, a common technique used to improve performance and availability, can also introduce security vulnerabilities if not properly configured. In MySQL and MariaDB, replication can be used to distribute the database load across multiple servers, improving performance by offloading read operations to replica servers. However, if replication is not set up with proper security measures, it can lead to unauthorized access to the replicated data. For example, an unsecured replication channel can allow malicious actors to intercept sensitive data as it is replicated between servers. DBAs should always ensure that replication traffic is encrypted using SSL/TLS connections and that access to replication streams is restricted to trusted hosts. Additionally, configuring proper user permissions on replica servers is crucial to prevent unauthorized access to sensitive data in the replication process.

Another security implication of performance tuning involves the adjustment of the InnoDB storage engine. Performance tuning often involves changing the configuration of the InnoDB buffer pool, adjusting log file sizes, or optimizing transaction handling to improve throughput and reduce I/O operations. However, these changes can also affect the durability and integrity of the data. For example, adjusting the innodb_flush_log_at_trx_commit parameter for performance optimization can reduce disk I/O, but it can also increase the risk of data loss in the event of a system crash. Similarly, reducing the frequency of log flushing to improve performance may expose the system to potential data corruption or loss. Therefore, when tuning InnoDB for better performance, DBAs must ensure that the changes do not compromise the durability of data or increase the risk of undetected data corruption.

Monitoring and logging are also vital areas where performance tuning intersects with security concerns. To achieve optimal performance, DBAs often configure logging settings to reduce overhead, such as disabling certain logs or limiting the amount of logged information. However, disabling critical logs, such as the general query log or error log, can make it harder to detect suspicious activity or identify security incidents. Proper logging is essential for identifying potential security breaches or unauthorized access attempts. When optimizing for performance, it is crucial not to compromise the level of logging required for effective security monitoring. DBAs should configure logging to capture necessary events without introducing excessive overhead, ensuring that both performance and security needs are met.

Finally, when tuning MySQL or MariaDB for performance, DBAs must ensure that their changes do not introduce new vulnerabilities through misconfiguration. Performance tuning often involves tweaking low-level settings and fine-tuning complex parameters that can have a significant impact on the system's overall behavior. Misunderstanding the implications of certain settings or making overly aggressive performance adjustments can inadvertently expose the system to security risks. Therefore, it is important to thoroughly understand the security implications of each performance tuning change and conduct comprehensive testing to ensure that the database continues to function securely while meeting performance objectives.

The relationship between performance tuning and security is one of careful balance. DBAs must prioritize performance improvements while maintaining robust security practices to protect sensitive data and ensure the integrity of the system. While it is tempting to push the boundaries of performance tuning, ensuring that the system remains secure at all times must be an integral part of the optimization process. By carefully considering the security implications of performance tuning changes, DBAs can create an environment that performs well while safeguarding the system against vulnerabilities and attacks.

Optimizing the MySQL and MariaDB Network Stack

Optimizing the network stack in MySQL and MariaDB is an essential component of improving database performance, especially in environments where the database handles a high volume of queries or operates in a distributed setup. The network stack plays a critical role in the communication between clients and the server, as well as between multiple nodes in a replicated or clustered database setup. Slow or inefficient network communication can introduce significant delays, affecting the responsiveness of the database and the user experience. Properly tuning the network stack can reduce latency, improve throughput, and ensure the efficient transfer of data across the system, which is particularly important for applications that rely on real-time data access.

The first step in optimizing the MySQL and MariaDB network stack is to understand how network communication works in these systems. When a client makes a request, the database server processes the request and sends the results back over the network. If the server is experiencing network congestion, high latency, or limited bandwidth, the response time will increase, leading to slower query performance. Several factors can influence network performance, including hardware limitations, server settings, and the configuration of the underlying operating system's network stack. By optimizing these factors, DBAs can ensure that the network infrastructure supports the database's needs efficiently.

One of the primary parameters that impact MySQL and MariaDB network performance is the max_connections setting, which determines how many concurrent client connections the database can handle. In environments with high traffic, increasing the value of max_connections allows the database to handle more simultaneous connections, reducing the chances of clients being blocked or queued. However, setting this parameter too high without proper resource allocation can lead to resource exhaustion, as each connection consumes CPU, memory, and network bandwidth. To optimize the connection handling, DBAs should ensure that the max_connections setting is aligned with the available server resources and anticipated load. Additionally, DBAs should monitor connections regularly to ensure that connection limits are not being exceeded, which can cause performance degradation.

Another key parameter for optimizing network performance in MySQL and MariaDB is the net_buffer_length setting, which determines the size of the buffer used for network communication. The larger the net_buffer_length, the more data can be transmitted per packet, reducing the overhead of multiple smaller packets and improving the efficiency of network communication. However, setting this value too high can increase memory usage, especially in systems that handle many connections concurrently. DBAs must find the right balance between optimizing data transmission and managing memory usage effectively. Adjusting the net_buffer_length should be done in conjunction with other network-related settings to ensure optimal performance across the entire network stack.

The wait_timeout and interactive_timeout parameters also play a crucial role in network performance. These settings control how long a connection can remain idle before it is closed by the server. For applications that make frequent but short-lived connections, setting an appropriate value for these timeouts can help free up resources that would otherwise be wasted on idle connections. However, setting the timeouts too low can result in frequent disconnects and reconnections, which introduces overhead and can reduce application performance. By tuning these parameters based on the expected connection patterns, DBAs can improve both network efficiency and system resource usage.

In addition to adjusting MySQL and MariaDB parameters, optimizing the operating system's network stack can also have a significant impact on performance. Network latency and throughput can be affected by the operating system's buffer sizes, the type of network interfaces used, and the settings for network congestion control. For example, increasing the size of the operating system's TCP send and receive buffers can allow MySQL or MariaDB to transmit more data with each packet, reducing the number of packets needed to transfer large amounts of data. This can be particularly useful for high-throughput applications that require the transfer of large result sets or bulk data operations. Adjusting the tcp_rmem and tcp_wmem parameters at the operating system level allows for fine-tuning the network buffer sizes, which can directly improve MySQL and MariaDB's network performance.

Another important consideration for optimizing the MySQL and MariaDB network stack is the use of SSL/TLS encryption for secure connections. While encryption ensures that data is transmitted securely over the network, it also introduces some overhead due to the encryption and decryption processes. For high-performance applications, the encryption overhead can be significant, especially when dealing with large volumes of data. DBAs should consider using optimized encryption algorithms, such as AES, and configure the SSL/TLS settings to use the most efficient options for their environment. Additionally, in scenarios where encrypted connections are not strictly necessary, DBAs can evaluate whether disabling SSL/TLS encryption for internal or trusted connections would result in better performance, reducing the overhead of the encryption process.

In distributed database environments, such as those involving replication or clustering, network performance becomes even more critical. In MySQL and MariaDB, replication can be configured to distribute database updates across multiple nodes, improving both availability and scalability. However, replication introduces additional network traffic as changes made on the master node are transmitted to the replica servers. The speed and efficiency of this replication process are highly dependent on the network infrastructure. To optimize replication performance, DBAs should ensure that replication traffic is encrypted and that the replication channels are properly configured to minimize latency and network congestion. Using tools like Percona XtraBackup to streamline replication and minimize the amount of data being transmitted over the network can also help improve replication speed.

Network topology and the physical network infrastructure also play a significant role in optimizing the MySQL and MariaDB network stack. In geographically distributed environments, where the database is accessed by clients or replicas across different data centers or regions, network latency can become a significant factor. To reduce the impact of latency, DBAs can place database servers closer to the clients or use content delivery networks (CDNs) or edge caching mechanisms to reduce the distance between the client and the database server. Additionally, selecting high-performance network interfaces, such as 10 GbE or higher, can significantly improve the throughput and reduce network congestion, ensuring that the database can handle large volumes of traffic efficiently.

Monitoring network performance is an ongoing task that allows DBAs to detect and address issues before they affect database performance. Tools such as MySQL Enterprise Monitor, Percona Monitoring and

Management (PMM), or other third-party monitoring solutions provide detailed insights into the database's network performance. By regularly tracking metrics like network latency, throughput, and connection counts, DBAs can identify any signs of network congestion, high latency, or resource exhaustion and take proactive steps to address these issues. Regular monitoring allows for the early detection of network-related performance problems, enabling DBAs to fine-tune the network stack and adjust the database configurations to optimize performance.

Ultimately, optimizing the MySQL and MariaDB network stack is an essential aspect of database performance management. By configuring the right parameters, optimizing the operating system's network settings, and leveraging high-performance network hardware, DBAs can reduce latency, improve throughput, and ensure that the network infrastructure supports the database's performance needs. In high-traffic, distributed, or high-availability environments, a well-optimized network stack can significantly improve the overall efficiency and responsiveness of the database, ensuring that it can handle even the most demanding workloads. The ongoing monitoring and adjustment of the network stack are crucial to maintaining optimal performance as network conditions and traffic patterns evolve over time.

InnoDB File-Per-Table vs. Shared Tablespace: Pros and Cons

In MySQL and MariaDB, the InnoDB storage engine provides two distinct approaches for managing table data storage: file-per-table and shared tablespace. Each approach has its own set of advantages and drawbacks that can impact database performance, management, and scalability. Understanding these two methods and their implications on database operations is crucial for database administrators (DBAs) to optimize their systems and make informed decisions about how to structure their database storage. The choice between using file-per-table or shared tablespace depends on various factors, such as performance requirements, backup strategies, and resource management needs.

The file-per-table approach stores each InnoDB table in its own individual tablespace, which is a separate file on the disk. This method is enabled by default in newer versions of MySQL and MariaDB and offers several advantages over the shared tablespace approach. One of the most significant benefits of file-per-table is that it provides better isolation between tables. Because each table is stored in its own file, operations on one table do not directly impact the performance or resource usage of other tables in the system. This can be particularly useful in environments with large databases, where one table may have heavy usage while others are relatively idle. If tables are stored in separate files, a heavy read or write load on one table does not affect the I/O performance of other tables in the system, which helps in maintaining overall performance.

Another advantage of the file-per-table method is improved disk space management. Since each table is stored in its own separate file, it is easier to monitor and manage disk usage on a per-table basis. If one table grows significantly in size, it can be monitored and managed independently of others. For example, large tables can be moved to a different disk or partition if necessary, without affecting the storage or performance of other tables. This provides greater flexibility in managing disk space, particularly for applications that involve large, growing datasets. Furthermore, when dropping or truncating a table, the file-per-table approach ensures that disk space is immediately reclaimed, as the table's file is deleted or truncated. In contrast, shared tablespaces can retain unused space even after table data is removed, making it more difficult to recover disk space efficiently.

File-per-table also facilitates improved performance for certain types of queries. With separate files for each table, the I/O operations associated with reading or writing data to a table are more predictable and localized to the file corresponding to that table. This can reduce contention for disk resources when multiple tables are being accessed concurrently. Additionally, since each table has its own dedicated file, InnoDB can more efficiently manage the buffer pool, reducing the chance of data from one table affecting the cache for another table. This can lead to better memory utilization and more efficient query processing.

On the other hand, shared tablespace uses a single common tablespace file, known as the system tablespace, where all InnoDB tables are stored. This method has been the default behavior in older versions of MySQL and MariaDB and has its own set of advantages. One key benefit of the shared tablespace is that it simplifies the management of tables. With all tables stored in the same file, the number of individual files on the filesystem is reduced, making it easier to manage and back up the database. Since there is only one large tablespace file, there is less overhead in managing multiple files for each table, which can be beneficial in simpler environments where ease of management is a priority.

Shared tablespaces can also be advantageous in certain backup scenarios. When using shared tablespaces, the entire database can be backed up in one go, which is more efficient for certain types of backup strategies. Backing up a single large tablespace file can be faster and more straightforward than backing up numerous individual files, especially in environments where the number of tables is very high. For example, for systems with many small tables that do not require individual management, the shared tablespace approach can simplify the backup process by reducing the need to handle multiple table files separately. Additionally, since shared tablespaces use a single file, it can be easier to manage consistency when performing database backups, as all data is stored in a single location.

However, the shared tablespace approach also comes with certain drawbacks, especially in terms of performance and flexibility. One of the primary disadvantages is the potential for performance degradation due to contention for disk resources. Since all tables are stored in a single file, heavy usage of one table can negatively impact the performance of other tables that share the same space. For example, if a large query on one table causes a high volume of disk I/O, it can lead to increased latency for other queries accessing different tables in the same tablespace. This contention can become more pronounced in multi-user environments, where numerous queries are executed simultaneously, causing I/O bottlenecks that affect the overall responsiveness of the database system.

Another disadvantage of shared tablespaces is that they make disk space management more difficult. Since all tables share the same file, it can be harder to isolate and track the storage usage of individual tables. If one table grows disproportionately, it may consume more space in the tablespace than desired, which can lead to fragmentation within the tablespace. This fragmentation can result in inefficient storage usage, where free space is scattered across the tablespace, making it harder for InnoDB to allocate space for new data. Moreover, when dropping or truncating tables, the freed space is not immediately reclaimed, which can cause the shared tablespace file to grow unnecessarily, leading to wasted disk space. This can be particularly problematic for databases with frequent schema changes, as it requires periodic maintenance and optimization to recover space effectively.

The shared tablespace approach also has limitations in terms of scalability. As the number of tables in the system grows, managing a single large tablespace file can become cumbersome. If the tablespace file becomes too large, it may take longer to perform operations such as backups, restores, or file manipulations. Additionally, the increased size of the shared file can increase the risk of data corruption in the event of a failure, as all tables rely on the integrity of that single file.

Choosing between file-per-table and shared tablespace depends on the specific needs and characteristics of the database environment. In high-traffic systems or environments with large, growing datasets, file-per-table offers better performance, flexibility, and disk space management. The isolation provided by separate tablespaces makes it easier to manage performance, as individual tables can be optimized and managed independently. On the other hand, shared tablespace may be suitable for simpler environments where ease of management and backup simplicity are more important than fine-grained control over disk usage or performance. For systems with many small tables or those that prioritize centralized management, shared tablespaces can simplify administration and backup processes.

In the end, the decision to use file-per-table or shared tablespace depends on the specific workload, system architecture, and administrative needs. By understanding the pros and cons of each approach, DBAs can make informed decisions that align with their performance goals, resource availability, and long-term scalability considerations.

Managing Auto-Increment Keys and Performance Considerations

Auto-increment keys are a fundamental feature in MySQL and MariaDB, providing a convenient way to generate unique identifiers for rows in a database table automatically. They are often used as primary keys to uniquely identify records and to ensure that each entry in the table has a distinct and easily accessible identifier. While auto-increment columns are generally efficient and convenient, managing them effectively is crucial for maintaining database performance, particularly in large-scale systems where the volume of data and the rate of inserts can have significant impacts on performance.

One of the primary benefits of using auto-increment keys is their ability to provide a simple and effective mechanism for generating unique identifiers without requiring manual intervention. When a new row is inserted into a table, the auto-increment column is automatically assigned the next available number, ensuring that each record has a unique key. This is particularly useful in environments where new data is continuously being added, and there is a need for a reliable way to generate unique identifiers without the risk of duplication or error.

However, despite their simplicity and usefulness, auto-increment keys can introduce performance challenges under certain conditions. One of the main concerns with auto-increment columns is the potential for contention and locking issues. When a large number of rows are inserted into a table simultaneously, the auto-increment counter may become a bottleneck, as each insert operation requires the database to obtain the next available value for the auto-increment column. In high-traffic systems, where numerous clients or processes are inserting data concurrently, this can lead to delays as each insert waits for the auto-increment value to be assigned. This contention can be particularly problematic when the auto-increment key is used as a primary key, as it may also be involved in index management, leading to further delays and performance degradation.

To mitigate these issues, it is essential to consider the configuration of the auto-increment counter. In MySQL and MariaDB, the auto-increment counter is typically stored in the table's metadata and is updated with each insert operation. By default, the auto-increment counter is incremented by 1, but this can be adjusted using the auto_increment_increment and auto_increment_offset system variables. The auto_increment_increment variable controls the step size between consecutive auto-increment values, and the auto_increment_offset variable controls the starting point for the counter. By adjusting these values, DBAs can reduce contention by distributing the auto-increment values across multiple threads or processes, ensuring that inserts can proceed more efficiently without waiting for the counter to be updated.

For example, in a multi-master replication setup, where multiple nodes are inserting data concurrently, using different auto_increment_offset values for each node can prevent conflicts between the auto-increment values generated on each server. This strategy ensures that each server generates a unique set of auto-increment values, avoiding the need for synchronization between the servers and reducing the potential for contention. Similarly, adjusting the auto_increment_increment value to a higher step size can reduce the number of times the auto-increment counter needs to be updated, further improving insert performance.

In addition to adjusting the auto-increment counter, managing the underlying indexes that are associated with the auto-increment column is also critical for optimizing performance. Since auto-increment columns are often used as primary keys, they are usually indexed by default. While this is generally beneficial for query performance, it can lead to performance degradation if the table is frequently updated or if the auto-increment key is heavily used in foreign key relationships. When the auto-increment key is updated or modified, the associated index must be updated as well, which can introduce overhead. This is especially true in tables with a large number of rows or in systems that experience a high rate of insert operations. To optimize performance, DBAs should consider the size of the table and the frequency of updates and inserts when designing indexes. In some cases, it may be beneficial to use a different indexing strategy, such as using a composite index or using a non-clustered index, to minimize the overhead of index maintenance.

Another performance consideration for auto-increment keys is the impact on storage. Auto-increment columns typically use integer data types, such as INT or BIGINT, to store the generated values. While these data types are efficient, they can consume a significant amount of storage space, especially in tables with a large number of rows. Over time, as the number of rows in the table increases, the storage requirements for the auto-increment key can become significant. This is particularly true if the table is using a BIGINT data type for the auto-increment column, which can consume 8 bytes per row. DBAs should carefully consider the data type used for the auto-increment column and ensure that it is appropriate for the expected size of the table. In many cases, using an INT data type may be sufficient, as it provides a large enough range for most use cases while consuming less storage space.

In systems where performance is critical, especially in high-throughput environments, using auto-increment keys for distributed systems can introduce additional challenges. For example, in sharded database architectures, where data is distributed across multiple nodes or clusters, managing auto-increment keys becomes more complex. Since each shard may require its own set of unique keys, coordinating auto-increment values across shards can become cumbersome. In such cases, it may be beneficial to use UUIDs (universally unique identifiers) instead of traditional auto-increment keys. UUIDs provide a unique identifier across all shards, eliminating the need for coordination between nodes and avoiding issues with contention. However, using UUIDs introduces its own performance considerations, as UUIDs are larger than integers and can increase the size of indexes, potentially leading to slower query performance. DBAs must weigh the trade-offs between using auto-increment keys and UUIDs based on the specific needs of the application and the database architecture.

Another technique for improving performance when using auto-increment keys is to optimize table partitioning. In large databases, partitioning can help distribute the data across multiple physical storage locations, improving query performance and reducing contention. By partitioning tables that use auto-increment keys, DBAs can spread the inserts across different partitions, reducing the likelihood of contention for the auto-increment counter and improving insert performance. Partitioning can also make it easier to manage large tables by allowing for more efficient backups, archiving, and data retrieval. However, partitioning requires careful design and consideration of the partitioning key, as it can introduce additional complexity and overhead if not done correctly.

Managing auto-increment keys effectively is essential for optimizing the performance of MySQL and MariaDB databases, particularly in high-traffic environments where insert operations are frequent. By adjusting the configuration of the auto-increment counter, managing indexes, optimizing storage, and considering alternative strategies such as UUIDs or table partitioning, DBAs can ensure that the auto-increment keys do not become a bottleneck. With the right approach, auto-increment keys can continue to provide a simple and efficient mechanism for generating unique identifiers while maintaining optimal database performance across large and complex systems.

Managing Transactions and Isolation Levels in MySQL and MariaDB

Transactions and isolation levels are foundational concepts in MySQL and MariaDB, ensuring that databases can handle concurrent operations safely while maintaining data integrity. A transaction is a logical unit of work that contains one or more SQL operations, such as inserts, updates, or deletes, which are executed as a single entity. The primary goal of transactions is to guarantee that these operations either all succeed or all fail together, ensuring the consistency of the database. At the same time, the database must handle multiple transactions executing concurrently, which can lead to conflicts or anomalies. The way MySQL and MariaDB handle these conflicts is largely determined by the isolation level, which defines the extent to which the operations of one transaction are isolated from others.

The ACID properties—Atomicity, Consistency, Isolation, and Durability—form the foundation of transaction management in

MySQL and MariaDB. Atomicity ensures that a transaction is treated as a single unit, meaning that all operations within the transaction must succeed for the transaction to be committed. If any operation fails, the entire transaction is rolled back, leaving the database in a consistent state. Consistency ensures that a transaction moves the database from one valid state to another. Isolation determines how the operations in one transaction are isolated from other transactions, and Durability guarantees that once a transaction is committed, its effects are permanent, even in the event of a system crash.

MySQL and MariaDB support four isolation levels: READ UNCOMMITTED, READ COMMITTED, REPEATABLE READ, and SERIALIZABLE. Each level defines a different balance between performance and data consistency, and choosing the right level depends on the specific needs of the application and the system's workload. The default isolation level in MySQL and MariaDB is REPEATABLE READ, which strikes a balance between consistency and concurrency by preventing non-repeatable reads, where a transaction reads a value and then finds that the value has been modified by another transaction before the transaction completes.

At the lowest level, READ UNCOMMITTED allows transactions to see uncommitted changes made by other transactions. This isolation level can result in "dirty reads," where a transaction reads data that might later be rolled back. While this isolation level provides the best performance because transactions are not blocked, it compromises data integrity and consistency, making it unsuitable for most applications that require reliable data.

READ COMMITTED is the next level up in terms of isolation, where transactions can only see committed data. This level prevents dirty reads but still allows "non-repeatable reads," where a value read by one transaction may change if another transaction commits a modification. While this isolation level offers a compromise between consistency and performance, it may still introduce anomalies in applications where it is crucial to maintain a consistent view of data throughout the duration of a transaction.

REPEATABLE READ, the default isolation level in MySQL and MariaDB, prevents dirty reads and non-repeatable reads, ensuring that once a transaction reads a value, it will see the same value for the duration of the transaction. This level ensures that the data remains consistent and avoids anomalies like non-repeatable reads. However, it still allows "phantom reads," where a transaction may see different sets of rows if another transaction inserts, updates, or deletes rows that meet the query's criteria. This isolation level provides a stronger guarantee of consistency, but it can lead to higher contention and blocking between transactions, which can degrade performance in high-concurrency environments.

The highest isolation level, SERIALIZABLE, ensures the highest level of consistency by making transactions behave as if they were executed serially, meaning that no other transaction can access the data that the current transaction is working on. This isolation level prevents dirty reads, non-repeatable reads, and phantom reads. However, the tradeoff is significant in terms of performance, as it can introduce heavy locking, reduce concurrency, and increase the likelihood of deadlocks. SERIALIZABLE is most useful in scenarios where absolute consistency is required and where the performance impact can be tolerated, such as in financial systems or applications with strict consistency requirements.

Choosing the appropriate isolation level requires careful consideration of the application's needs. For example, applications that perform heavy reads and can tolerate some level of inconsistency may benefit from using READ COMMITTED or even READ UNCOMMITTED, as these levels allow for more concurrency and better performance. On the other hand, applications that require strict data consistency, such as banking systems or inventory management applications, may require the stronger guarantees provided by REPEATABLE READ or SERIALIZABLE.

When configuring isolation levels, it is important to understand the potential impact on performance. Lower isolation levels, such as READ UNCOMMITTED, allow for greater concurrency and better performance, but they also increase the risk of anomalies and inconsistent data. Higher isolation levels, like SERIALIZABLE, provide stronger consistency guarantees but come at the cost of reduced concurrency and increased locking. As such, DBAs need to balance the application's requirements for data consistency with the performance and scalability of the database. For instance, in an e-commerce application where users are browsing products, the performance benefit of using READ COMMITTED may outweigh the risk of occasional non-repeatable reads, whereas in an accounting application, the need for consistency might justify the use of REPEATABLE READ or even SERIALIZABLE.

In addition to isolation levels, DBAs must also consider transaction management and configuration settings that impact the behavior of transactions. For example, the innodb_flush_log_at_trx_commit parameter controls the frequency with which transaction logs are flushed to disk. Setting this parameter to 1 ensures that transaction logs are written to disk after every commit, providing the highest durability guarantee but potentially slowing down performance. Setting it to 2 or 0 reduces the frequency of disk writes, which can improve performance but at the cost of losing some durability in the event of a crash.

Another consideration is the management of transaction locks. InnoDB uses row-level locking to allow multiple transactions to operate concurrently while minimizing contention. However, if a transaction holds a lock for too long, it can block other transactions, leading to delays or even deadlocks. To avoid this, DBAs should monitor lock contention and optimize transaction duration by keeping transactions as short as possible. Additionally, it is essential to properly index tables to minimize the need for full table scans, which can lead to unnecessary locking.

Monitoring tools, such as the SHOW ENGINE INNODB STATUS command, can provide insights into the behavior of transactions, including lock waits, transaction history, and deadlock occurrences. By reviewing these details regularly, DBAs can identify performance bottlenecks related to transaction management and make adjustments to the system configuration or query execution plans.

The management of transactions and isolation levels in MySQL and MariaDB is a crucial aspect of database administration. By understanding how different isolation levels affect data consistency and performance, and by configuring the system to align with the specific needs of the application, DBAs can ensure that transactions are handled efficiently while maintaining the integrity and reliability of the database. Effective transaction management requires a balanced approach that considers both the consistency guarantees required by the application and the performance demands of the system.

Implementing Full-Text Search and Tuning Performance

Full-text search is a powerful feature in MySQL and MariaDB that enables efficient searching of large text-based data within a database. This functionality is especially useful for applications that deal with unstructured data, such as articles, product descriptions, and user-generated content. By indexing and querying text fields with full-text search capabilities, MySQL and MariaDB can offer a fast and effective way to retrieve relevant data based on text matching. However, implementing full-text search and tuning its performance require a nuanced approach to ensure optimal results, especially as the size of the dataset grows.

Full-text search in MySQL and MariaDB works by creating a full-text index on one or more columns, typically those containing textual data. This index stores information about the words in the text, which allows for faster searching than scanning the entire content of each row. When a query is executed with a MATCH and AGAINST clause, MySQL or MariaDB can use the full-text index to quickly find the rows that contain the words or phrases being searched for. Unlike regular indexes that work on exact matches, full-text indexes allow for searching partial matches and ranking the relevance of results based on factors like word frequency and position within the text.

One of the most important aspects of full-text search is the creation of the full-text index. To implement full-text search in MySQL or MariaDB, you must first create a full-text index on the relevant column(s) using the CREATE INDEX or ALTER TABLE statement. The full-text index is built on the specified text columns, and once it is created, you can use the MATCH and AGAINST syntax in SQL queries to perform searches. However, full-text search is only available on certain storage engines in MySQL and MariaDB, with InnoDB and

MyISAM being the most common. MyISAM, in particular, has historically been preferred for full-text indexing because of its simple and fast implementation, though InnoDB has added support for full-text indexing starting with MySQL 5.6 and MariaDB 10.0.

Once a full-text index is in place, performance optimization becomes crucial, especially when dealing with large datasets. One important factor in tuning full-text search performance is the size of the index itself. Full-text indexes can become very large, especially when indexing large amounts of text data. As the index grows, the time it takes to perform searches can increase. To mitigate this, it is important to keep the size of the full-text index manageable. One way to do this is by carefully selecting which columns to index. For example, indexing text fields that contain only a few words or are rarely searched can be wasteful, while focusing on columns that are frequently searched can help optimize the index size. Additionally, DBAs can use the BOOLEAN MODE or WITH QUERY EXPANSION options to refine search queries and reduce the load on the index.

In addition to managing the index size, optimizing the MATCH and AGAINST query syntax is important for improving performance. The MATCH statement performs a full-text search against one or more indexed columns, and the AGAINST clause specifies the search query. By default, full-text search in MySQL and MariaDB uses a natural language search mode, which ranks results based on relevance and can be affected by factors such as stop words, word frequency, and the minimum word length. Tuning the minimum word length can have a significant impact on search performance. For example, by default, MySQL and MariaDB may not index words shorter than a specified length (usually 4 characters). This can be adjusted by modifying the ft_min_word_len variable, but DBAs should be cautious, as reducing the minimum word length can lead to larger index sizes and longer query times.

Another important consideration in full-text search performance is the handling of stop words. Stop words are common words such as "the," "and," or "is," that are typically ignored during the search process because they appear too frequently to be useful in distinguishing relevant results. However, the default list of stop words may not be ideal for all applications. In MySQL and MariaDB, the list of stop words can be customized to suit specific needs. By modifying the ft_stopword_file configuration, DBAs can provide a custom list of stop words, or even disable the use of stop words altogether. This can be particularly useful in situations where stop words may be significant to the search context, such as when searching for common terms in product descriptions or specific jargon in technical documents.

Another key factor in full-text search performance is the use of IN BOOLEAN MODE. This mode allows for more advanced search capabilities, such as supporting logical operators like + (must have) and - (must not have) to refine search results. Using IN BOOLEAN MODE allows users to specify more complex search queries, such as searching for documents that must contain certain words while excluding others. While Boolean mode can be highly effective for precise searches, it can also introduce additional complexity and performance overhead if used improperly. It is important to monitor the impact of Boolean searches, particularly when executing queries with many terms or complex conditions, as they can increase the processing time required to match results against the index.

Aside from the database-specific configurations, the underlying hardware also plays a significant role in the performance of full-text search. Disk speed and available memory directly affect how quickly the database can read from and write to the full-text index. In particular, solid-state drives (SSDs) can significantly improve the speed of indexing and querying by reducing the latency associated with disk I/O operations. Similarly, ensuring that the database server has enough memory to hold the index in the buffer pool can reduce the need for disk accesses, improving the performance of full-text searches. For large datasets, partitioning the table or splitting large text fields into smaller, more manageable segments can also improve performance by reducing the size of individual full-text indexes and making queries more efficient.

Another optimization consideration is the frequency of full-text index updates. In databases with high rates of insertions, updates, or deletions, the full-text index may need to be rebuilt periodically to maintain optimal performance. For example, in a blog or article database where new content is frequently added, the full-text index can become out of sync with the underlying data if it is not updated regularly. MySQL and MariaDB offer options for optimizing the frequency of index maintenance, including adjusting the frequency of index updates or using tools like OPTIMIZE TABLE to rebuild indexes and reclaim space. Regular index maintenance ensures that queries continue to execute efficiently as the data set grows.

When implementing and tuning full-text search in MySQL or MariaDB, it is important to assess the specific needs of the application and carefully manage the trade-offs between search performance, index size, and query complexity. By selecting the right columns for indexing, fine-tuning query syntax, adjusting database and server configurations, and regularly maintaining indexes, DBAs can ensure that full-text search remains an effective and efficient tool for retrieving relevant data. Proper performance tuning not only enhances the responsiveness of full-text searches but also ensures that the database can scale effectively as data volumes increase.

Query Rewriting Techniques to Improve Efficiency

Query rewriting is an essential technique for optimizing database performance, particularly when dealing with complex or inefficient queries. In MySQL and MariaDB, queries that are poorly written or inefficiently structured can result in slow execution times, excessive resource consumption, and suboptimal performance for the entire database system. Rewriting queries not only improves the efficiency of individual queries but can also have a significant impact on the overall performance of the database by reducing resource contention, minimizing I/O overhead, and speeding up data retrieval. The process of query rewriting involves analyzing the query structure and modifying it to achieve better execution plans, faster response times, and reduced load on the database.

One of the first techniques in query rewriting is ensuring that the query uses the most efficient access paths for data retrieval. One of the most common causes of inefficiency in SQL queries is the failure to use indexes effectively. Indexes are essential for speeding up data retrieval, particularly for large tables. However, many queries fail to take advantage of available indexes due to improper use of WHERE clauses, joins, or filtering conditions. By analyzing query execution plans with the EXPLAIN command, DBAs can determine whether the query is using indexes effectively or performing full table scans unnecessarily. If indexes are not being used, the query can be rewritten to incorporate indexed columns in the WHERE or JOIN conditions, improving efficiency by reducing the amount of data that needs to be scanned.

For example, consider a query that retrieves data from a large table with a condition on a non-indexed column. The query can be rewritten to add an index on that column or adjust the query to filter data using a different indexed column. In some cases, it may be more efficient to break down a complex query into multiple smaller queries, each targeting a specific subset of data. This can reduce the amount of work required for each query and improve overall performance.

Another common inefficiency arises from the use of SELECT * in queries. While using SELECT * can be convenient, it often results in the retrieval of more data than necessary. This can lead to unnecessary network overhead and increased memory usage, especially if the table has many columns, many of which are not needed for the query result. By explicitly specifying the required columns in the SELECT clause, the query can be rewritten to fetch only the necessary data, reducing both the amount of data transferred and the time spent processing the query.

In some cases, complex subqueries can be rewritten into more efficient join operations. Subqueries, especially correlated subqueries, can result in multiple passes through the data, which can be slow and inefficient. Rewriting a correlated subquery as a join can often result in a significant performance improvement. For instance, instead of using a subquery to find rows that match a condition, a query can be rewritten to join the relevant tables and apply the condition directly in the join clause. This eliminates the need for the database to process the subquery multiple times and can result in faster query execution.

Using EXISTS instead of IN is another common query rewriting technique to improve performance. The IN operator in SQL can be inefficient when used with subqueries, particularly when the subquery returns a large result set. The EXISTS operator, on the other hand, can be more efficient because it stops processing as soon as a match is found. By replacing an IN clause with EXISTS in queries that involve subqueries, DBAs can reduce the amount of data processed and improve query execution times.

Another technique for improving query efficiency is the use of proper join types. MySQL and MariaDB support different types of joins, including INNER JOIN, LEFT JOIN, and RIGHT JOIN, each with different performance characteristics. In some cases, using the wrong type of join can result in unnecessary data being retrieved or incorrect results being returned. For example, if a query includes a LEFT JOIN when an INNER JOIN would suffice, the database may perform unnecessary work by retrieving rows from the left table even if no matching rows exist in the right table. By carefully considering the appropriate join type for each query, DBAs can optimize query performance and reduce the amount of data being processed.

Query rewriting also involves eliminating redundant operations. For example, if a query includes a WHERE condition that checks the same column multiple times or performs the same operation repeatedly, this redundancy can be eliminated by simplifying the query structure. Removing unnecessary calculations or repetitive filtering conditions can reduce the computational overhead and speed up query execution. Similarly, queries that involve GROUP BY clauses can often be optimized by rewriting them to use more efficient aggregation techniques or by reducing the number of rows being grouped through better filtering in the WHERE clause.

In addition to these general techniques, query rewriting can also involve optimizing the use of aggregate functions. For instance, instead of calculating aggregates for large result sets and then filtering the results, the query can be rewritten to apply the filtering condition first and then perform the aggregation. This can significantly reduce the amount of data being processed and improve query performance. In some cases, it may be beneficial to use indexed views or materialized views to store the results of complex aggregations, reducing the need to recalculate the aggregates each time the query is executed.

In some cases, it may be beneficial to optimize queries by considering the size of the data being queried. For instance, when querying large tables, DBAs can ensure that the query includes appropriate filtering conditions to limit the amount of data being retrieved. Additionally, for large datasets, partitioning the table can improve query performance by reducing the number of rows that need to be scanned for each query. By optimizing queries to only target relevant partitions, DBAs can significantly reduce the query execution time.

Another important consideration when rewriting queries is the use of temporary tables. For complex queries that require multiple intermediate steps or involve large result sets, using temporary tables can help break down the query into smaller, more manageable pieces. Temporary tables can be used to store intermediate results, which can then be processed more efficiently in subsequent steps. This can help avoid performing complex operations on large datasets all at once, which can overwhelm the system and lead to slow query performance.

Finally, the use of query caching can also play a role in improving the efficiency of repeated queries. MySQL and MariaDB support query caching, which stores the results of a query in memory for quick retrieval the next time the same query is executed. For frequently executed queries that return the same result set, enabling query caching can eliminate the need to re-execute the query and reduce the overall load on the database. However, it is important to note that query caching is only effective for read-heavy workloads and queries that do not change frequently, as cache invalidation can introduce overhead in write-heavy environments.

Query rewriting is a powerful tool for optimizing database performance. By carefully analyzing the structure of SQL queries and applying various rewriting techniques, DBAs can significantly improve query efficiency. Whether by optimizing joins, eliminating redundant operations, or reducing the size of the result set, query rewriting helps ensure that MySQL and MariaDB databases perform at their best. By continuously refining queries and adopting best practices for query optimization, DBAs can ensure that their databases handle large volumes of data efficiently, providing a fast and responsive experience for end users.

Scaling MySQL and MariaDB for High Traffic Applications

Scaling MySQL and MariaDB for high traffic applications is a critical consideration for ensuring that these databases can handle large volumes of concurrent connections, complex queries, and massive datasets without degrading performance. High traffic applications often experience significant fluctuations in load, and as user activity increases, database systems must be able to scale efficiently to accommodate this demand. Scaling a database is not a simple task, as it involves multiple layers of optimization, from hardware configurations to query optimization and distributed database architecture. By carefully planning and implementing the right scaling techniques, DBAs can ensure that MySQL and MariaDB can deliver high availability, fast response times, and reliable performance even in the most demanding environments.

The first step in scaling MySQL and MariaDB for high traffic applications is to evaluate the architecture and hardware resources required to support the anticipated load. In many cases, scaling begins with vertical scaling, which involves increasing the capacity of the database server itself. Vertical scaling typically involves adding more CPU cores, increasing memory, or expanding disk space to accommodate a higher volume of traffic and data. While vertical scaling can be effective in the short term, it has its limitations, as there is only so much capacity that can be added to a single server before it becomes a bottleneck. Therefore, for long-term scalability and to handle very high traffic, horizontal scaling or distribution strategies must also be considered.

Horizontal scaling, also known as database sharding, involves distributing data across multiple database instances or nodes. MySQL and MariaDB offer various approaches to horizontal scaling, such as replication and clustering, which allow data to be spread across multiple servers. In a replication setup, a master database is used for write operations, and multiple slave databases are used for read operations. This type of setup can significantly offload read-heavy workloads from the master server, improving overall performance. By distributing read queries across multiple replicas, the database can handle more traffic without compromising response times. However, write operations are still constrained by the master server's capacity, so scaling write operations requires additional strategies.

For write-heavy applications, clustering and multi-master replication provide more robust solutions. In MariaDB, for example, the Galera Cluster allows for synchronous multi-master replication, where each node in the cluster can handle both read and write operations. This ensures that each node remains in sync with the others, and as a result, the system can scale horizontally by adding more nodes to handle the increasing load. With a Galera Cluster, write operations are distributed across multiple nodes, reducing the load on any single server and improving overall database availability and fault tolerance. This setup also provides high availability, as nodes in the cluster can automatically take over if one of the nodes fails, minimizing downtime for the application.

Beyond basic scaling techniques, performance tuning and query optimization play an essential role in handling high traffic applications. No matter how many database servers are deployed, inefficient queries or suboptimal schema designs can still create significant bottlenecks. One of the first areas to address is indexing. Proper indexing can dramatically speed up query performance by reducing the amount of data that needs to be scanned. However, adding too many indexes can slow down insert operations and increase the storage requirements. DBAs should carefully analyze which columns are frequently queried and create indexes on those columns, ensuring that indexes are used efficiently without negatively impacting write performance.

In addition to indexing, optimizing query performance is critical when scaling MySQL and MariaDB. Complex queries involving joins, subqueries, or aggregations can become performance bottlenecks under high load. By analyzing the execution plans of queries using the EXPLAIN command, DBAs can identify inefficient operations and find ways to rewrite queries to improve performance. Common techniques for query optimization include simplifying joins, avoiding unnecessary subqueries, and limiting the number of rows retrieved by using more selective WHERE clauses. In some cases, breaking down complex queries into smaller, more manageable subqueries can help reduce the strain on the database.

Caching is another powerful technique for improving the performance of high traffic applications. Caching reduces the number of queries that need to be executed by storing frequently accessed data in memory. MySQL and MariaDB both support query caching, which stores the results of SELECT queries so that they can be quickly retrieved the next time the same query is executed. This is particularly useful for read-heavy applications where the same data is requested multiple times. For even greater caching efficiency, application-level caching systems such as Redis or Memcached can be used to cache entire query results or frequently accessed objects in memory. These systems reduce the load on the database by serving cached data for repeated queries, allowing the database to focus on handling more complex operations.

Another aspect of scaling MySQL and MariaDB for high traffic applications is ensuring that the system can handle large datasets efficiently. As the volume of data grows, DBAs need to implement strategies like partitioning to improve query performance. Table partitioning involves dividing a large table into smaller, more manageable pieces, based on certain criteria such as range, list, or hash. This allows the database to work with smaller chunks of data, improving query performance by reducing the number of rows that need to be scanned. Partitioning can also help optimize data management tasks like backups, as smaller partitions can be backed up independently, reducing the time and resources required for backup operations.

Load balancing is another critical component of scaling MySQL and MariaDB for high traffic applications. In a multi-server setup, load balancing ensures that incoming queries are evenly distributed across the available servers. This helps prevent any single server from becoming overwhelmed with requests and ensures that the system can handle spikes in traffic more efficiently. Load balancers can be configured to distribute read queries to replica servers and write queries to the master server or use more advanced load-balancing algorithms to determine which server should handle a given request. Properly configured load balancing can improve both performance and high availability by ensuring that the database infrastructure remains responsive even under heavy load.

To support high availability and prevent downtime, database clustering and replication solutions like Galera Cluster, Percona XtraDB Cluster, or MySQL Group Replication can be employed. These solutions allow multiple database nodes to work together in a fault-tolerant manner, providing redundancy and automatic failover capabilities. By implementing clustering and replication, DBAs can ensure that the database remains available even if a node fails. This is particularly important for high traffic applications that require minimal downtime and consistent performance.

Monitoring is a vital part of maintaining performance as MySQL and MariaDB are scaled for high traffic applications. Regular monitoring of key performance indicators (KPIs) such as query execution time, replication lag, disk I/O, and memory usage allows DBAs to identify potential bottlenecks and optimize resource usage. Tools like Percona Monitoring and Management (PMM) or MySQL Enterprise Monitor can provide valuable insights into the health of the database and alert DBAs to any issues that may arise. Continuous monitoring helps ensure that the database can handle increasing traffic without sacrificing performance, making it easier to identify and address performance issues proactively.

Scaling MySQL and MariaDB for high traffic applications requires a multifaceted approach that includes horizontal scaling, query optimization, efficient resource management, caching, and robust monitoring. By carefully selecting the right scaling techniques and implementing performance optimization strategies, DBAs can ensure that their databases remain responsive, reliable, and capable of handling increasing traffic loads as their applications grow. This comprehensive approach to database scaling is essential for high-traffic environments where performance, high availability, and scalability are critical to the success of the application.

Using Galera for Synchronous Replication in MariaDB

Galera is a high-performance, synchronous multi-master replication solution for MySQL and MariaDB that provides true synchronous replication across multiple nodes in a cluster. It enables all nodes to be writable, unlike traditional replication methods where a single master node handles writes while one or more slave nodes only handle read requests. This setup provides both high availability and load balancing capabilities for databases. By ensuring that data is immediately synchronized across all nodes, Galera ensures that every node in the cluster has an up-to-date copy of the data, making it a perfect solution for high-availability applications where downtime is not acceptable.

At the heart of Galera's operation is its synchronous replication mechanism. In traditional asynchronous replication, a change made to the master node is not immediately reflected on the slave nodes; instead, it may take some time for the changes to propagate. This can lead to data inconsistencies between the master and the slaves, particularly in high-traffic environments where changes are frequent. With Galera, however, when a transaction is committed on one node, it is replicated to all other nodes in the cluster in real-time before the transaction is considered fully committed. This ensures that all nodes have the same data at the same time, which eliminates replication lag and prevents the risk of reading outdated data from a slave.

The synchronous nature of Galera replication comes with a few key characteristics that make it stand out from traditional master-slave replication. One of the most significant advantages is the ability to perform multi-master replication. In a typical setup, only the master node can handle write operations, while the slave nodes are read-only. This creates a potential bottleneck, especially for write-heavy applications. With Galera, every node in the cluster can accept both read and write operations, which improves scalability by distributing the write load across multiple nodes. This also increases the fault tolerance of the system, as any node can take over as the master in the event of a failure, reducing the risk of a single point of failure.

In addition to providing multi-master replication, Galera ensures consistency across all nodes in the cluster. The primary mechanism behind this consistency is the use of a certification protocol that is applied to every transaction. When a transaction is executed on a node, the changes are first replicated to the other nodes, which then verify the transaction against the current state of the data. If there is a conflict, such as when two nodes attempt to modify the same piece of data simultaneously, Galera uses a mechanism called "certification-based conflict resolution" to ensure that only one of the transactions is committed and the other is rolled back. This ensures that the data remains consistent across all nodes, even in the presence of simultaneous writes.

The synchronous replication model used by Galera has several important benefits, particularly for high-availability and high-performance applications. One of the main advantages is the elimination of replication lag. In traditional asynchronous replication setups, there is always a delay between when a write is made on the master and when it is reflected on the slave. This delay can lead to issues such as data inconsistency and stale reads, particularly when a failure occurs. With Galera, since all nodes are kept in sync in real-time, the risk of reading outdated data is minimized, and applications can be confident that they are always working with the most current version of the data.

Another key benefit of using Galera is its automatic failover capability. If one node in the cluster goes down, the other nodes can continue processing transactions without any disruption to the application. This automatic failover is essential for high-availability applications, as it ensures that the database remains operational even if one or more nodes fail. Galera's automatic node join and re-sync features ensure that any new or recovering nodes can quickly catch up with the rest of the cluster without manual intervention. This simplifies database management and minimizes downtime during failures or maintenance.

To set up Galera for synchronous replication in MariaDB, the first step is to install and configure the Galera software on all nodes in the cluster. Galera operates on the InnoDB storage engine, which is the default for MariaDB, so no additional configuration is required for

InnoDB-based tables. Once Galera is installed, the nodes in the cluster need to be configured to communicate with each other. This involves configuring the wsrep_cluster_address parameter in the MariaDB configuration file (my.cnf) to specify the addresses of the other nodes in the cluster. Additionally, other Galera-specific parameters, such as wsrep_cluster_name and wsrep_node_name, need to be set to identify the cluster and individual nodes.

Once the configuration is complete, the nodes can be started, and the cluster will automatically begin synchronizing. Each node in the cluster will participate in the certification process and will be able to accept both read and write operations. If a node fails or is added to the cluster, Galera ensures that the remaining nodes continue to function, and the new or recovering node will be brought up to speed automatically. This ensures that the database remains highly available and resilient to node failures.

While Galera's synchronous replication model provides many benefits, it is important to be aware of its limitations. One potential drawback of synchronous replication is the increased latency compared to asynchronous replication. Since transactions must be certified and replicated across all nodes before being committed, there is a slight increase in the time it takes for a transaction to be fully committed. However, this latency is typically minimal and can be managed by optimizing the hardware and network infrastructure. Additionally, since every node must be involved in the transaction certification process, the performance of the system can be impacted if the cluster size grows too large or if the nodes are geographically distributed. In such cases, it may be necessary to fine-tune Galera's configuration or scale the infrastructure to maintain optimal performance.

Another consideration is the impact of write-heavy workloads on the cluster. While Galera supports multi-master replication, write-heavy applications may still face challenges in scaling due to the synchronous nature of the replication process. Each write operation must be replicated to all nodes before it is committed, which can introduce delays if the system is not properly tuned or if the network bandwidth between nodes is insufficient. In such cases, strategies such as horizontal scaling, sharding, or the use of read-write splitting can be employed to distribute the load and improve performance.

In terms of monitoring and management, tools such as the Galera Cluster's own status commands or third-party monitoring solutions like Percona Monitoring and Management (PMM) can be used to track the health of the nodes, replication status, and performance metrics. Monitoring the cluster's health is essential to ensure that all nodes are functioning properly, and to identify and address issues such as network latency, replication lag, or node failures before they impact the application.

Galera provides a powerful solution for implementing synchronous replication in MariaDB, offering advantages in terms of high availability, data consistency, and automatic failover. By using Galera, organizations can scale their databases horizontally while maintaining a high level of data integrity across all nodes in the cluster. While there are considerations regarding latency and write-heavy workloads, with proper configuration and tuning, Galera can significantly improve the resilience and performance of MariaDB databases in high-traffic environments.

Performance Tuning for Stored Procedures and Triggers

Stored procedures and triggers are powerful tools in MySQL and MariaDB that help encapsulate business logic, automate tasks, and ensure that data integrity is maintained. They allow for the execution of predefined SQL code in response to specific actions or events. However, while they provide significant advantages in terms of automation and consistency, poorly optimized stored procedures and triggers can severely impact database performance, especially in high-traffic environments. Effective performance tuning of these elements is essential to ensure that they enhance, rather than hinder, the overall efficiency of the database.

Stored procedures are precompiled SQL statements that can be executed with a single call, often used to encapsulate repetitive tasks, complex logic, or operations that involve multiple steps. Triggers, on the other hand, are automatic actions that are executed in response to events such as INSERT, UPDATE, or DELETE operations on a table. Although both stored procedures and triggers are extremely useful, they can become performance bottlenecks if they are not designed or optimized properly.

One of the first steps in tuning stored procedures and triggers is to minimize the amount of work they perform. Stored procedures can often become inefficient when they include complex logic, loops, or multiple queries that can be simplified. For example, nested queries or large numbers of conditional checks within stored procedures can significantly increase execution times. In these cases, DBAs should examine the logic to determine if it can be streamlined. Breaking down complex stored procedures into smaller, more manageable parts can often improve both readability and performance. Furthermore, stored procedures that involve multiple queries should be analyzed to determine if they can be reduced to fewer queries or if subqueries can be optimized for better performance.

For triggers, the performance impact can be even more pronounced since triggers are executed automatically in response to database events. If a trigger involves complex logic or multiple steps, it can significantly slow down the operation that caused the trigger to fire. This is especially problematic in high-volume tables, where triggers may be fired frequently. To optimize trigger performance, DBAs should avoid placing complex logic or heavy operations inside the trigger itself. Instead, it may be more efficient to move this logic into stored procedures or application-level code, where more flexibility and control are available. Additionally, triggers should be designed to execute as quickly as possible to minimize the time spent on the operations they are designed to monitor.

Another common performance issue with stored procedures and triggers is the excessive use of cursors. While cursors can be useful for iterating through result sets, they are typically slower than set-based operations, which process multiple rows of data at once. When tuning stored procedures or triggers, DBAs should avoid the use of cursors whenever possible. Instead, they should try to rewrite the logic to use more efficient set-based SQL operations, such as JOINs, subqueries, or batch updates. Set-based operations allow the database engine to optimize the query execution, resulting in better performance than processing each row individually with a cursor.

Indexing is another critical aspect of optimizing stored procedures and triggers. When queries within stored procedures or triggers perform searches, lookups, or joins on large tables, the lack of proper indexing can cause significant slowdowns. In these cases, DBAs should ensure that the appropriate indexes are in place for the columns being queried. For example, when a stored procedure or trigger involves a SELECT statement that filters data on a specific column, an index on that column can speed up the lookup process. However, it is important to balance the need for indexes with the potential overhead of maintaining them during inserts, updates, and deletes. Too many indexes can slow down write operations, so DBAs should aim to create indexes that strike a balance between read and write performance.

The use of variables within stored procedures and triggers also plays a role in performance. While variables can make stored procedures more flexible, excessive use of them, especially when they are repeatedly set or modified within loops, can create performance issues. To optimize performance, it is essential to limit the use of variables to only what is necessary for the task at hand. Minimizing the number of variables and avoiding unnecessary recalculations can help reduce the execution time of both stored procedures and triggers.

Another tuning technique is to ensure that stored procedures and triggers are as lightweight as possible. For example, stored procedures that return large result sets should be avoided unless absolutely necessary. Returning large amounts of data from a stored procedure can lead to excessive memory usage and slow response times. Instead, DBAs can consider alternative methods such as returning only the necessary columns or rows or using pagination to limit the amount of data returned at once. Similarly, triggers should avoid performing operations that generate large result sets, as they may significantly slow down the triggering operation.

One overlooked aspect of performance tuning for stored procedures and triggers is managing transactions effectively. When a stored procedure or trigger involves multiple SQL operations, it is important to ensure that transactions are used correctly. For example, when performing a series of updates within a stored procedure, using an explicit transaction ensures that the updates are atomic and consistent. However, if transactions are left open for too long, they can lock tables and slow down other operations. DBAs should ensure that transactions are kept as short as possible to minimize the impact on database performance. This can be achieved by committing or rolling back transactions as soon as the necessary operations are complete.

In some cases, the execution time of stored procedures and triggers can be affected by the underlying server configuration. For example, the max_allowed_packet configuration setting in MySQL or MariaDB can limit the size of the data that can be sent between the client and server. If a stored procedure or trigger is attempting to send large amounts of data, it may be necessary to adjust this setting to accommodate the larger packets. Additionally, server settings related to memory allocation, such as the sort_buffer_size or read_buffer_size, can impact the performance of queries within stored procedures. DBAs should monitor the system's resource usage and adjust these settings accordingly to ensure that the database engine has enough memory to execute the procedures and triggers efficiently.

The use of profiling and monitoring tools is essential for identifying performance issues with stored procedures and triggers. MySQL and MariaDB provide built-in tools such as the SHOW PROFILE command and the performance_schema to track the execution time and resource consumption of queries, including those executed within stored procedures and triggers. By using these tools, DBAs can pinpoint specific areas where stored procedures or triggers are causing performance issues and make targeted optimizations.

In high-traffic environments, performance tuning for stored procedures and triggers becomes even more important. As the volume of transactions increases, poorly optimized stored procedures and triggers can quickly become a bottleneck, slowing down the entire system. By streamlining the logic, optimizing queries, minimizing unnecessary operations, and carefully managing resources, DBAs can ensure that stored procedures and triggers contribute positively to the performance of the database system. Properly tuned stored procedures and triggers can help maintain the efficiency and reliability of a high-traffic database, ensuring that the system can handle increasing loads without sacrificing performance or stability.

Advanced Monitoring with MySQL Enterprise Tools

Effective monitoring is crucial to maintaining the health and performance of MySQL databases, particularly in large-scale or high-traffic environments. While basic monitoring can track essential parameters such as query response times and resource usage, more advanced monitoring capabilities are needed to gain a comprehensive understanding of database performance. MySQL Enterprise Tools provide advanced monitoring features that enable database administrators (DBAs) to track a wide array of metrics, detect performance issues early, and gain deeper insights into the database's behavior. These tools help optimize database operations, enhance efficiency, and maintain high availability, ensuring that MySQL databases remain responsive and reliable.

MySQL Enterprise Monitor is one of the primary tools used for advanced monitoring. It offers real-time tracking and in-depth analysis of various MySQL and MariaDB server metrics, including query performance, server resource usage, replication health, and storage efficiency. Through a centralized interface, DBAs can easily access detailed performance data, set up alerts, and monitor the health of individual instances or clusters. The Enterprise Monitor helps DBAs spot potential issues before they affect the performance of the database, minimizing downtime and ensuring smooth database operations.

One of the key benefits of MySQL Enterprise Monitor is its ability to track query performance across the entire system. The tool captures detailed data about query execution times, resource consumption, and frequency. This data allows DBAs to identify slow or resource-intensive queries and optimize them accordingly. By using the query analysis feature, DBAs can detect patterns in query execution and pinpoint problem areas. For example, queries that involve inefficient joins, missing indexes, or unnecessary subqueries can be identified and rewritten for better performance. Moreover, the monitor provides insights into which queries are consuming the most CPU or I/O resources, allowing DBAs to prioritize their optimization efforts.

MySQL Enterprise Tools also provide advanced replication monitoring capabilities. In distributed database environments, where replication is used to synchronize data across multiple servers, keeping track of replication health is essential. Replication lag can occur when the slave nodes fall behind the master node, leading to stale or inconsistent data. The Enterprise Monitor allows DBAs to monitor replication lag in real time and set up alerts for when it exceeds predefined thresholds. This enables immediate corrective actions to be taken, ensuring that replication remains consistent and that the database continues to operate as expected. Additionally, the tool tracks replication errors, such as failed transactions or replication conflicts, and provides detailed information to help DBAs quickly address any issues.

Another important feature of MySQL Enterprise Tools is its ability to monitor server resources, such as CPU usage, memory consumption, disk I/O, and network activity. These metrics are critical for understanding the overall health of the database server and identifying potential bottlenecks. MySQL Enterprise Monitor continuously tracks these parameters and generates reports on resource usage trends over time. By analyzing this data, DBAs can identify underutilized resources that can be reallocated to improve performance or over-utilized resources that may require optimization. For instance, high CPU usage could indicate the need for better query optimization or the addition of more processing power, while excessive disk I/O could suggest the need for more efficient indexing or a faster storage subsystem.

The ability to monitor and manage storage efficiency is another valuable feature of MySQL Enterprise Tools. Over time, databases can accumulate unused or fragmented data, leading to inefficient storage usage and reduced performance. The Enterprise Monitor provides insights into disk space usage and helps identify tables that are growing excessively large or consuming more storage than expected. DBAs can also use the tool to monitor InnoDB buffer pool usage, identifying potential issues related to memory allocation and optimizing buffer pool settings to reduce disk I/O and improve query response times.

Moreover, the tool can track the growth of binary logs and slow query logs, allowing DBAs to implement proper log rotation and ensure that logs do not consume excessive storage space.

For large-scale environments with multiple MySQL instances, MySQL Enterprise Tools offer centralized monitoring across all instances. DBAs can track performance metrics for individual servers or entire clusters from a single interface. This centralized view simplifies the management of complex database environments and enables DBAs to identify systemic issues that may affect multiple instances. For example, if several nodes in a cluster are experiencing high replication lag or excessive resource usage, the Enterprise Monitor can provide insights into the underlying causes, such as hardware limitations or configuration issues. By consolidating data from all database instances, MySQL Enterprise Tools help DBAs proactively manage the health of the entire infrastructure and maintain consistent performance across all nodes.

MySQL Enterprise Monitor also includes the ability to set up custom alerts and notifications based on specific performance thresholds. For example, DBAs can configure alerts for slow queries, high replication lag, or resource overutilization. These alerts can be sent via email, SMS, or other communication channels, ensuring that DBAs are immediately informed of any issues that require attention. The flexibility of custom alerts allows DBAs to tailor their monitoring approach to the unique needs of their environment, ensuring that critical issues are addressed in a timely manner.

In addition to monitoring the performance of MySQL databases, MySQL Enterprise Tools provide security monitoring features. Security is an increasingly important aspect of database management, and MySQL Enterprise Monitor helps DBAs track potential vulnerabilities or misconfigurations that could expose the database to risks. The tool provides insights into user access patterns, privilege changes, and failed login attempts, allowing DBAs to detect potential security threats early. By analyzing these security metrics, DBAs can ensure that proper access control policies are in place and take corrective actions if any security issues arise.

MySQL Enterprise Tools also include capabilities for backup monitoring and management. Regular backups are essential for ensuring data durability and recovery in case of failure, but poorly managed backups can lead to performance issues or, worse, data loss. The Enterprise Monitor tracks backup status, providing alerts for any failures or delays in the backup process. This enables DBAs to ensure that backups are completed successfully and within the desired time frame. Additionally, the tool helps manage backup schedules, ensuring that backups are performed during off-peak hours to minimize the impact on database performance.

MySQL Enterprise Tools provide an essential suite of features for DBAs looking to implement advanced monitoring and performance optimization in their MySQL and MariaDB environments. With the ability to track query performance, monitor replication health, optimize resource usage, manage storage efficiency, and ensure security and backup integrity, these tools give DBAs the insights needed to proactively maintain the health of their database systems. By leveraging MySQL Enterprise Tools, organizations can ensure high availability, improve performance, and mitigate risks, allowing their MySQL databases to handle even the most demanding workloads with confidence.

Managing Server Configuration Files for Optimal Performance

Managing server configuration files is an essential aspect of ensuring that MySQL and MariaDB perform optimally under varying workloads. The server configuration file, typically named my.cnf in MySQL and MariaDB, contains numerous settings that control how the database engine behaves, how it utilizes system resources, and how it interacts with clients. Adjusting these parameters appropriately can have a significant impact on performance, scalability, and resource utilization. Understanding how to configure the server to suit specific needs, whether for read-heavy or write-heavy workloads, high concurrency, or complex transactions, is crucial for DBAs to maintain a stable and high-performing database system.

The my.cnf file is divided into sections, each of which controls specific aspects of the server's behavior. These sections include global server settings, database engines, and various performance-related parameters. To get the best performance, DBAs must fine-tune these settings based on the workload characteristics and hardware resources of the server. While some defaults are suitable for general use, most production environments will benefit from custom configurations that take full advantage of the available system resources.

One of the first areas to focus on when tuning MySQL or MariaDB is memory allocation. The database engine uses several memory-related parameters to control how memory is allocated for operations such as query execution, indexing, caching, and buffering. The most critical memory parameters include innodb_buffer_pool_size, key_buffer_size, sort_buffer_size, and read_buffer_size. For InnoDB, the innodb_buffer_pool_size is perhaps the most important. It determines how much memory is allocated to the InnoDB buffer pool, which caches data and indexes to reduce disk I/O. The larger the buffer pool, the more data can be stored in memory, reducing the need for frequent disk accesses and improving overall performance. However, allocating too much memory to the buffer pool at the expense of other system processes can lead to memory exhaustion, so it is essential to find a balance based on the available system memory.

Similarly, the key_buffer_size parameter controls memory allocation for MyISAM tables, which is another storage engine used in MySQL and MariaDB. Although InnoDB is the default in recent versions, MyISAM is still widely used in some applications. The key_buffer_size determines the amount of memory allocated for indexing operations. For servers that use MyISAM tables heavily, increasing the key buffer size can improve performance by speeding up index-related operations. However, allocating too much memory to the key buffer can compete with the memory used by InnoDB or other system processes, leading to inefficiencies.

Another important memory-related parameter is the sort_buffer_size. This parameter controls the amount of memory allocated for sorting operations during query execution. If a query involves sorting large result sets, increasing the sort buffer size can improve performance by allowing the entire sort operation to take place in memory. However, allocating too much memory to sorting buffers can negatively affect overall system performance if many concurrent connections are using large sort buffers simultaneously.

Disk I/O is often one of the biggest bottlenecks in database performance, and as such, optimizing disk usage is essential for ensuring fast data retrieval. MySQL and MariaDB offer various settings that help manage disk I/O, such as the innodb_log_file_size, innodb_flush_log_at_trx_commit, and innodb_io_capacity parameters. The innodb_log_file_size controls the size of the log files used for transactional writes. Increasing the log file size can reduce the frequency of disk writes and improve performance for write-heavy workloads. However, larger log files require more time to flush to disk, and improper sizing can lead to slower recovery times in the event of a crash.

The innodb_flush_log_at_trx_commit setting determines when changes to the transaction log are written to disk. Setting this to 1 (the default) ensures that changes are written to disk after every commit, providing the highest durability but also introducing disk I/O overhead. In environments where write performance is more critical than absolute durability, DBAs may consider setting this value to 2 or 0 to reduce disk I/O. However, this comes at the cost of potentially losing transactions in the event of a server crash.

The innodb_io_capacity parameter defines the I/O capacity of the system, indicating the maximum number of I/O operations InnoDB can perform per second. Tuning this parameter based on the system's actual disk I/O capabilities can help improve the performance of I/O-intensive operations such as bulk inserts or complex queries.

Query performance can be optimized by adjusting settings related to the query cache and thread management. The query_cache_size and query_cache_type parameters control the query cache, which stores the results of SELECT queries to speed up repeated queries. For read-heavy workloads, enabling and appropriately sizing the query cache can significantly improve performance by reducing the number of queries that need to be executed. However, for write-heavy environments, enabling the query cache may lead to performance degradation due to cache invalidation, so it is essential to carefully consider whether query caching is beneficial for the specific workload.

Thread management parameters, such as max_connections, thread_cache_size, and wait_timeout, also play an important role in managing performance in high-traffic environments. The max_connections setting determines the maximum number of concurrent connections that the server will accept. In high-traffic applications, this value must be large enough to accommodate peak connection loads. However, setting this value too high can lead to excessive memory usage and unnecessary contention for resources. The thread_cache_size controls the number of threads that can be cached to handle incoming client connections efficiently. Increasing this value can reduce the overhead of creating new threads for each incoming connection, but if set too high, it can lead to memory wastage.

Additionally, the wait_timeout and interactive_timeout parameters control how long connections can remain idle before they are closed. Reducing these values can help free up resources from idle connections and improve overall performance in environments with many short-lived connections. However, setting these values too low may result in frequent connection terminations, which could impact performance, especially for applications that require long-lasting connections.

In addition to adjusting specific configuration parameters, DBAs must also take the operating system's resources into account when configuring MySQL or MariaDB. System-level settings, such as CPU affinity, memory overcommit handling, and disk I/O scheduling, can all influence database performance. Configuring the server's OS to prioritize MySQL-related processes can ensure that the database has sufficient resources available for optimal operation. Additionally, utilizing faster storage systems, such as SSDs, for the database files and logs can significantly reduce disk latency and improve performance.

Regular monitoring is also a vital component of managing configuration files for optimal performance. DBAs should continuously track key performance metrics, including query execution time, resource utilization, disk I/O, and cache hit rates, to assess the impact of configuration changes. Tools like MySQL Enterprise Monitor or

Percona Monitoring and Management (PMM) provide insights into database performance and can help identify areas where further tuning is necessary.

Managing MySQL or MariaDB server configuration files is an ongoing task that requires careful attention to both system resources and workload characteristics. By adjusting memory allocations, optimizing disk I/O, tuning thread management, and managing query performance, DBAs can ensure that their database systems are configured to handle high traffic, large datasets, and complex queries efficiently. Through continuous monitoring and iterative adjustments, the database can be kept in an optimal state, ensuring high performance, scalability, and reliability.

Using Optimizer Hints to Influence Query Execution

Optimizer hints in MySQL and MariaDB are a powerful mechanism for influencing the execution plan of SQL queries. When the database engine processes a query, it uses its internal optimizer to determine the most efficient way to execute the query, considering factors such as indexes, join methods, and query complexity. However, there are times when the optimizer's chosen plan may not be the most efficient for a particular use case. In such situations, optimizer hints can be used to override the default behavior and instruct the database to use a specific execution strategy. By strategically applying optimizer hints, DBAs and developers can fine-tune query performance, especially in complex or high-load environments.

Optimizer hints are special comments embedded within SQL queries that provide instructions to the query optimizer. These hints can influence various aspects of query execution, such as the choice of indexes, join methods, or the use of specific query optimizations. Optimizer hints are particularly useful when the query optimizer's automatic decisions lead to suboptimal execution plans, which can result in poor performance. In such cases, hints provide a way to guide the optimizer towards a more efficient execution strategy, ensuring that queries are processed in the most optimal manner.

One of the most commonly used optimizer hints is the index hint. Indexes are crucial for speeding up data retrieval, and MySQL and MariaDB typically select the most appropriate index for a query based on available indexes and query structure. However, the optimizer's choice may not always align with the user's expectations, especially if there are multiple indexes that could be used for the same query. In such cases, index hints can be applied to force the query optimizer to use a specific index. For example, the USE INDEX hint instructs the optimizer to use a particular index when processing a query. Similarly, the IGNORE INDEX hint tells the optimizer to ignore certain indexes that might otherwise be considered. These hints can be particularly useful when dealing with complex queries or when the optimizer is choosing a suboptimal index that leads to excessive scanning or inefficient performance.

Another useful hint is the FORCE INDEX hint, which forces the optimizer to use a specific index, even if the optimizer deems another index to be more efficient. This hint can be useful in scenarios where the query performance is sensitive to the choice of index and the optimizer's default decision does not yield the best performance. For instance, in cases where an index is selective and highly efficient for a specific query, but the optimizer is choosing a less efficient index, using the FORCE INDEX hint ensures that the query executes with the desired index, avoiding potential performance degradation caused by a suboptimal plan.

In addition to index-related hints, MySQL and MariaDB support hints that influence the join methods used in a query. Joins are often a critical part of query execution, and the choice of join algorithm can have a significant impact on performance. MySQL and MariaDB support several join methods, including nested loops, hash joins, and sort-merge joins. The optimizer typically chooses the join method based on factors like the size of the tables, the presence of indexes, and the available memory. However, in some cases, forcing a specific join method can lead to better performance. The JOIN hint allows DBAs to specify which join method to use for particular tables in a query. For example, using a hash join might be more efficient than a nested loop join in certain scenarios, and a FORCE JOIN hint can be used to explicitly instruct the optimizer to use a hash join.

Similarly, the STRAIGHT_JOIN hint forces the optimizer to join tables in the order in which they are listed in the query. By default, the optimizer decides the most efficient order in which to join tables, which is generally based on factors like table size and available indexes. However, in certain cases, controlling the join order manually can improve performance, especially if the user has a good understanding of the data distribution and table sizes. The STRAIGHT_JOIN hint can be useful when the optimizer's join order leads to inefficient execution or when the user wants to ensure a specific join sequence.

Optimizer hints can also be used to control the query execution plan with respect to sorting operations. Sorting is a common operation in queries involving ORDER BY clauses, and the choice of sorting algorithm can significantly impact query performance, particularly when sorting large datasets. MySQL and MariaDB offer hints to control the sorting method used during query execution. The ORDER BY hint can be used to influence the sorting process, particularly when there are multiple ways to execute the sorting operation. For example, it may instruct the optimizer to use an in-memory sort instead of disk-based sorting, which is typically much faster. Optimizing sorting operations can lead to substantial improvements in query performance, particularly for queries that involve large result sets.

Another area where optimizer hints are particularly useful is in controlling the execution of subqueries. Subqueries are often used in complex queries to filter or aggregate data. However, subqueries can lead to inefficient execution, especially if they are correlated or return large result sets. The SUBQUERY hint allows users to control how subqueries are executed. For example, the hint can be used to instruct the optimizer to treat the subquery as a derived table or to optimize it as an independent query. By rewriting queries with subqueries and applying appropriate optimizer hints, DBAs can reduce unnecessary processing and improve the overall query execution time.

Optimizer hints can also be applied to control parallel execution in MySQL and MariaDB, particularly when dealing with large datasets or high-concurrency environments. Parallel execution allows the database to divide a query into smaller tasks and execute them concurrently, which can lead to faster processing times. However, parallel execution may not always be the most efficient approach for every query, depending on factors like data distribution and resource availability. The NO_PARALLEL hint can be used to disable parallel execution for specific queries, while the FORCE_PARALLEL hint can be used to explicitly enable parallel execution, even if the optimizer would otherwise avoid it. By controlling parallelism, DBAs can fine-tune query performance based on the characteristics of the query and the system's resource availability.

Although optimizer hints provide a powerful way to influence query execution, they should be used cautiously and judiciously. Overusing hints can lead to queries that are difficult to maintain and troubleshoot. The optimizer is generally quite good at choosing the most efficient execution plan, and manually overriding its decisions can sometimes result in suboptimal performance. Therefore, it is important to test the performance impact of any hints applied to queries and ensure that they lead to a real improvement. In many cases, the optimizer's default execution plan may be the most efficient, especially if the underlying data and schema are well-designed.

Using optimizer hints effectively requires a deep understanding of the query execution process and a solid knowledge of the database engine's inner workings. By leveraging optimizer hints strategically, DBAs and developers can gain fine-grained control over query execution, resulting in faster response times and improved overall performance. Proper use of optimizer hints can be a powerful tool in tuning MySQL and MariaDB queries, especially in complex, high-performance applications.

Troubleshooting Slow Replication in MySQL and MariaDB

Replication is an essential feature in MySQL and MariaDB, allowing data to be synchronized between a master (or primary) server and one or more slave (or replica) servers. This setup is crucial for ensuring high availability, distributing read load, and providing disaster recovery options. However, in some cases, replication may slow down, causing delays in data propagation between the master and its replicas. When replication becomes slow, it can lead to inconsistent data across servers, performance issues, and potentially significant downtime. Troubleshooting slow replication is vital to ensure that the system remains responsive and reliable.

The first step in troubleshooting slow replication is to identify the root cause of the issue. MySQL and MariaDB offer a variety of tools and status variables that provide insights into replication performance. One of the most useful tools for diagnosing replication problems is the SHOW SLAVE STATUS command. This command provides a wealth of information about the status of replication on the replica server, including details about the replication thread, replication lag, and errors. The key fields to pay attention to in the output of SHOW SLAVE STATUS include Seconds_Behind_Master, Relay_Log_Space, and Last_Error. If the value of Seconds_Behind_Master is large or increasing, it indicates that the replica server is lagging behind the master server, and further investigation is needed to determine the cause.

Replication lag can occur for a variety of reasons, and the first area to investigate is the system's I/O and disk performance. Replication involves two main threads on the replica server: the I/O thread, which reads binary logs from the master, and the SQL thread, which processes the events and applies them to the replica's data. If either thread is slow, replication can be delayed. One common reason for slow replication is insufficient disk I/O performance on the replica server. If the replica's disk is unable to keep up with the volume of replication data being written, it can result in lag. This can be particularly problematic if the master server is generating a high volume of write operations or if the replica is dealing with large transactions. Ensuring that the replica server has sufficient disk throughput, particularly if it's using traditional spinning hard drives rather than SSDs, can help resolve replication lag caused by disk bottlenecks.

Another important aspect to check is the replica's network connection to the master server. If the network link between the master and replica is unstable or slow, replication can suffer. Network latency or packet loss can delay the transmission of binary logs, leading to replication lag. In such cases, improving the network infrastructure, reducing network congestion, or relocating the replica closer to the master server can help mitigate replication delays. It's also important to ensure that the master server is not overwhelmed with too many connections, as this could impact the performance of the I/O thread, which depends on establishing a reliable connection to the master.

The configuration of the master server itself is another key factor in troubleshooting slow replication. If the master server is experiencing high load, slow replication may occur due to the excessive consumption of system resources. High CPU utilization, excessive disk I/O, or memory contention can slow down the generation of binary logs, which, in turn, causes delays in replication. Checking the master server's resource utilization, optimizing queries, and ensuring that it is not running excessive background processes can help alleviate replication issues. Additionally, ensuring that the binlog_format is set to ROW rather than STATEMENT can improve replication efficiency by reducing the complexity of the binary logs, especially in write-heavy environments.

Another potential cause of slow replication is the size of the relay log. The relay log is a temporary storage area on the replica where binary log events from the master are written before being processed by the SQL thread. If the relay log becomes too large, it can slow down replication. In such cases, the replica may not be able to process events quickly enough, leading to lag. DBAs should monitor the size of the relay log and consider increasing the size of the replica's innodb_buffer_pool_size or adjusting the relay_log_space_limit to prevent the relay log from growing excessively. It's also important to ensure that the replica has enough memory to efficiently store and process the relay log events.

Another factor contributing to slow replication is inefficient queries running on the replica. While the SQL thread is processing replication events, it may be competing for resources with other queries that are being executed on the replica server. This can cause the replication thread to be delayed, especially if resource-intensive queries or complex joins are running concurrently. Optimizing queries on the replica and ensuring that resource-heavy operations are scheduled during off-peak hours can help improve replication performance. Additionally, it's important to ensure that the replica's schema is optimized, with proper indexes in place, to reduce the load on the SQL thread when processing events.

The use of triggers, foreign keys, and stored procedures on the replica can also impact replication performance. These database features can add overhead to replication, especially when they introduce additional logic that must be executed during the replication process. Triggers, for instance, can slow down the SQL thread by executing additional operations on the replica each time a change is made. Similarly, foreign key constraints can cause delays, as they require additional checks during each replication event to maintain referential integrity. In high-traffic environments, minimizing the use of these features on the replica or disabling them altogether can reduce the replication load.

In some cases, replication may become slow due to the size of the data being replicated. Large transactions or bulk data changes on the master can cause delays in replication, particularly if the replica is struggling to apply the changes. One way to address this issue is to optimize the batch size of the transactions on the master server. For example, reducing the size of individual transactions can allow the replica to process changes more quickly. Alternatively, during periods of high load, DBAs may choose to temporarily stop or throttle replication to allow the replica to catch up before resuming normal operations.

Deadlocks between the I/O and SQL threads can also contribute to replication lag. If the I/O thread and the SQL thread attempt to access the same resources simultaneously, a deadlock can occur, causing replication to stall. To address deadlocks, DBAs should carefully review the replication process and ensure that the system is configured to handle concurrent access efficiently. Increasing the priority of the replication threads and ensuring that the replica server is well-balanced in terms of resource allocation can help reduce the likelihood of deadlocks.

In conclusion, troubleshooting slow replication in MySQL and MariaDB involves a multifaceted approach that takes into account disk I/O, network performance, master server configuration, query optimization, and resource contention. By carefully diagnosing the issue using tools like SHOW SLAVE STATUS, examining system resources, and optimizing queries and server configurations, DBAs can mitigate replication lag and ensure that the database operates efficiently. Regular monitoring and proactive maintenance are key to identifying replication issues early and preventing them from affecting the overall performance and availability of the database.

Advanced Table Optimizations for High-Volume Databases

In high-volume databases, where vast amounts of data are generated and queried daily, table optimizations become crucial for maintaining performance and scalability. Optimizing database tables is not just about creating indexes or tuning basic settings; it requires a deeper understanding of how MySQL and MariaDB process data, how table structure influences query execution, and how to balance the trade-offs between performance, storage efficiency, and maintainability. Advanced table optimization techniques are essential to handle large datasets, high traffic, and complex queries without sacrificing performance.

One of the fundamental principles in optimizing tables for high-volume environments is choosing the right storage engine. InnoDB is the default and most commonly used storage engine for MySQL and MariaDB due to its support for ACID compliance, transactions, and row-level locking. However, for certain use cases, other storage engines such as MyISAM or TokuDB might offer advantages in terms of read-heavy workloads or compression. InnoDB is highly versatile and optimized for high-concurrency environments, but for databases that primarily handle large read-heavy queries, evaluating the use of MyISAM or other engines optimized for specific workloads can provide performance benefits. Additionally, for environments with frequent writes and large-scale data inserts, using partitioning with InnoDB can enhance both performance and manageability.

Another key optimization technique for high-volume databases is careful indexing. Indexes are essential for speeding up data retrieval by reducing the amount of data that must be scanned during query execution. However, indexing can also have a downside, as it consumes additional storage and impacts the performance of write operations. When optimizing tables, it is important to ensure that indexes are used efficiently. This means creating indexes on columns that are frequently used in WHERE clauses or as part of joins but avoiding over-indexing, which can slow down insert and update operations. A critical part of index optimization is choosing the right type of index. For example, while B-tree indexes are ideal for equality and range queries, full-text indexes are better suited for searching text-based data.

For high-volume databases, composite indexes can be an effective way to speed up queries that filter or join on multiple columns. Composite indexes help avoid the need for multiple single-column indexes and can dramatically improve query performance by covering several columns in one index. However, creating composite indexes requires careful planning, as the order of the columns in the index matters. The columns that are most frequently used in filtering or sorting should be placed at the front of the composite index. It's also crucial to evaluate whether covering indexes—indexes that include all the columns needed by a query—can be used to reduce the need for accessing the table data altogether, further speeding up query execution.

Table partitioning is another powerful technique for optimizing high-volume databases. Partitioning involves splitting a large table into smaller, more manageable pieces while retaining the logical structure of the data. Each partition can be stored separately, and queries that target specific partitions can access only the relevant data, significantly improving performance. MySQL and MariaDB support various partitioning methods, such as range, list, hash, and key partitioning. Range partitioning is useful when data can be grouped by a specific range, such as dates, while hash partitioning is effective when distributing data evenly across multiple partitions. By partitioning large tables, databases can avoid full table scans and improve query performance, especially for time-series data or logs where data is naturally divided into time intervals.

To maximize table performance, it is important to consider the design of the database schema itself. Normalization plays a key role in organizing data efficiently, but in high-volume environments, it may be necessary to de-normalize certain parts of the schema to optimize query performance. De-normalization involves merging tables or adding redundant data to avoid expensive joins. While de-normalization can lead to faster queries, it comes at the cost of increased storage requirements and potential data consistency issues. It is a trade-off that should be carefully considered when designing tables for high-volume databases, especially when balancing the need for fast data retrieval with the overhead of maintaining data consistency.

Another area of optimization is the use of appropriate column data types. Choosing the right data type for each column is essential for both storage efficiency and query performance. For example, using a data type that is too large for the data being stored can unnecessarily consume storage space and impact performance. On the other hand, using a data type that is too small can lead to data truncation or overflow issues. It is crucial to select the most appropriate data type for each column based on the size and type of data it will hold. Additionally, ensuring that columns are appropriately indexed and minimizing the use of variable-length data types such as TEXT or BLOB when possible can prevent unnecessary overhead.

For tables that experience heavy insert and update operations, optimizing the handling of auto-increment values can also improve performance. Auto-increment columns are often used to generate unique identifiers for rows in a table, but the default behavior can lead to contention on a single value. To avoid this, using strategies such as setting the auto_increment_increment to a higher value or using UUIDs instead of sequential integers can distribute the load more evenly across the system. While UUIDs can increase storage requirements and indexing overhead, they can improve performance in environments where high concurrency is required.

Efficiently managing table fragmentation is another important optimization strategy for high-volume databases. Over time, as rows are inserted, updated, and deleted, tables can become fragmented, leading to slower query performance due to inefficient disk space usage. Regularly running the OPTIMIZE TABLE command helps defragment tables and reclaim unused space. This process reorganizes the physical storage of data, improving read and write performance. For InnoDB tables, this operation can also help optimize the performance of the buffer pool by reducing the number of disk reads required to retrieve data. While OPTIMIZE TABLE can be useful, it should be performed during off-peak hours or maintenance windows, as it can place significant load on the database.

Another key consideration in high-volume environments is the management of temporary tables. Temporary tables are often created during query execution to store intermediate results, but in high-traffic systems, their creation and management can become a bottleneck. Ensuring that temporary tables are created in memory rather than on disk can reduce the overhead associated with I/O operations. InnoDB uses memory-based temporary tables by default, but when the table exceeds a certain size, it is written to disk. Monitoring and adjusting the tmp_table_size and max_heap_table_size parameters can help control the size of in-memory temporary tables and reduce the frequency with which they are written to disk.

Lastly, effective use of query caching can significantly reduce the load on high-volume databases. MySQL and MariaDB offer query caching mechanisms that store the results of frequently executed queries. While query caching can speed up read-heavy applications, it is most effective when the database workload consists of a large number of repeated read operations. However, caching can be less effective in write-heavy environments, where cache invalidation and updates to the data require frequent invalidation of cached queries. DBAs should evaluate the cache hit ratio and adjust the query cache size accordingly. In environments with high traffic, using an external caching layer, such as Redis or Memcached, can provide better scalability and performance than relying solely on database-level query caching.

Optimizing tables in high-volume databases requires a multifaceted approach that involves careful schema design, indexing strategies, memory and disk optimizations, and appropriate configurations for handling high traffic. By applying these advanced techniques, DBAs can ensure that MySQL and MariaDB databases maintain high performance, scalability, and reliability, even as the volume of data and query load increases. Through ongoing monitoring, regular maintenance, and thoughtful adjustments, high-volume databases can continue to deliver fast, efficient responses to users and applications.

Using ProxySQL to Improve MySQL and MariaDB Performance

ProxySQL is a powerful, high-performance proxy layer for MySQL and MariaDB databases, designed to enhance their scalability, availability, and performance. By sitting between the application and the MySQL or MariaDB servers, ProxySQL acts as an intermediary that intelligently routes database queries, manages connections, and optimizes query handling. This allows ProxySQL to provide a range of performance improvements, including load balancing, query caching, query routing, and connection pooling. In environments where high availability and performance are paramount, ProxySQL can be a crucial tool for enhancing the efficiency of MySQL and MariaDB setups.

One of the most important features of ProxySQL is its ability to handle load balancing between multiple MySQL or MariaDB servers. In a typical database setup with replication, queries are often sent directly to the master server, resulting in a performance bottleneck as the system grows. ProxySQL addresses this by distributing read queries across multiple replica servers, reducing the load on the master server and improving the overall scalability of the system. ProxySQL can be configured to send write queries to the master server and read queries to replicas, ensuring that the system can handle high volumes of queries without overloading any individual server. The load balancing mechanism also provides fault tolerance, as traffic can be automatically rerouted to healthy nodes if one of the database servers fails.

Another significant benefit of using ProxySQL is its connection pooling capabilities. Connection pooling reduces the overhead associated with establishing and closing database connections, which can be particularly expensive in high-traffic environments. Instead of each application request opening and closing a new database connection, ProxySQL maintains a pool of persistent connections to the backend

MySQL or MariaDB servers. When a new query comes in, ProxySQL can quickly assign an existing connection from the pool, significantly reducing latency and improving response times. This is especially beneficial in applications that need to process many short-lived queries, as it avoids the repetitive overhead of establishing new connections for every request.

Query routing is another powerful feature provided by ProxySQL. In complex database environments, it is common to have different types of databases or multiple versions of MySQL or MariaDB running on different nodes. ProxySQL allows for advanced query routing strategies that can direct traffic to specific servers based on criteria such as the type of query, database schema, or even the client that is making the request. For example, ProxySQL can be configured to route read-only queries to replicas while routing write queries to the master server. This fine-grained control over query routing ensures that each query is sent to the most appropriate server, improving query performance and ensuring that resources are utilized efficiently.

Query caching in ProxySQL is another technique that can significantly improve the performance of MySQL and MariaDB setups. ProxySQL can cache the results of frequently executed read queries, reducing the need to repeatedly execute the same query on the backend servers. By caching query results in memory, ProxySQL can serve the results directly to the application without needing to hit the database, thus reducing load on the backend servers and improving response times. This is particularly beneficial for read-heavy applications, where the same queries are often executed multiple times. However, it is important to note that query caching in ProxySQL works best for read-only queries that do not change frequently. For write-heavy applications or environments with high data turnover, the cache may need to be cleared regularly to ensure that the data remains up to date.

Another critical area where ProxySQL shines is in its ability to provide query filtering and optimization. ProxySQL can be configured to analyze and optimize incoming queries before they reach the backend servers. It can be set up to block certain types of queries that are known to be inefficient or resource-intensive, such as those that involve full table scans or complex joins. Additionally, ProxySQL supports the use of query rewriting rules, which allow for the modification of queries to improve their efficiency. For example, ProxySQL can automatically convert SELECT queries that are known to be inefficient into more optimized queries, such as rewriting them to use indexed columns or converting joins to more efficient forms. This built-in query optimization feature can result in significant performance improvements, particularly for complex workloads.

ProxySQL also offers features to help manage high availability and failover scenarios. In a typical MySQL or MariaDB replication setup, if the master server goes down, the entire system can be disrupted, as the replicas are only readable and cannot process write queries. ProxySQL addresses this issue by automatically detecting when a master server becomes unavailable and rerouting traffic to a new master or another available server. This failover mechanism ensures that the system remains available even in the event of a server failure, minimizing downtime and preventing disruptions to the application. ProxySQL also supports multi-master replication setups, providing additional flexibility and fault tolerance in environments that require high availability.

Performance monitoring and diagnostics are key features of ProxySQL, helping DBAs identify and resolve performance issues quickly. ProxySQL provides real-time metrics on query execution, server load, and connection usage, allowing administrators to track the performance of individual queries and backend servers. This data can be used to identify bottlenecks, such as slow queries or high connection usage, and optimize the system accordingly. ProxySQL also supports the logging of queries, which allows for detailed analysis of query execution patterns and can be used to troubleshoot performance issues. Additionally, ProxySQL offers extensive support for monitoring backend MySQL or MariaDB servers, helping DBAs assess the health of the replication process, track server load, and identify any issues with replication lag.

The flexibility and extensibility of ProxySQL also contribute to its performance-enhancing capabilities. ProxySQL can be configured and customized to meet the specific needs of different environments. For example, administrators can create advanced routing rules to handle complex query traffic or adjust the configuration to optimize resource utilization based on the hardware and traffic patterns. ProxySQL can also be integrated with external monitoring tools to provide a more comprehensive view of system performance and resource utilization. The ability to fine-tune the proxy layer to meet specific workload demands ensures that ProxySQL can be tailored to provide optimal performance for a wide variety of applications and use cases.

Overall, ProxySQL offers a robust and highly flexible solution for improving the performance of MySQL and MariaDB databases. By acting as an intelligent proxy layer, it can balance read and write traffic, optimize query handling, reduce connection overhead, and ensure high availability. ProxySQL's advanced features, such as query caching, query routing, and failover management, make it an essential tool for scaling MySQL and MariaDB in high-traffic environments. For DBAs and developers looking to optimize the performance of their MySQL or MariaDB systems, ProxySQL provides a powerful solution that enhances both database efficiency and reliability.

MySQL and MariaDB Tuning for Virtualized Environments

Virtualized environments have become an essential part of modern IT infrastructure, offering flexibility, scalability, and resource efficiency. MySQL and MariaDB, being some of the most popular open-source relational database management systems, are often deployed within virtualized environments to leverage the benefits of virtualization. However, running MySQL or MariaDB on virtualized platforms introduces specific challenges that require specialized tuning to ensure optimal performance. Virtualization adds an extra layer of complexity, affecting various aspects of database performance, including CPU, memory, disk I/O, and network performance. Understanding how virtualization impacts MySQL and MariaDB performance and applying appropriate tuning techniques is crucial to maintaining high availability, responsiveness, and efficient resource usage.

One of the first areas to address when tuning MySQL or MariaDB for virtualized environments is CPU allocation. Virtual machines (VMs) typically share physical CPU resources with other VMs running on the same host. This can lead to CPU contention, particularly during high-traffic periods or when multiple VMs are running CPU-intensive processes. MySQL and MariaDB rely heavily on CPU resources for query processing, so ensuring that the database has access to sufficient processing power is critical. In virtualized environments, it is essential to assign adequate CPU cores to the VM running MySQL or MariaDB while avoiding over-committing CPU resources, which can lead to performance degradation. CPU over-commitment occurs when multiple VMs are allocated more virtual CPUs (vCPUs) than the host system can provide, resulting in CPU contention and slower query execution.

One effective way to optimize CPU usage in virtualized environments is to configure CPU affinity. CPU affinity allows the hypervisor to bind specific vCPUs to physical CPU cores, which can help reduce CPU context switching and improve performance. By ensuring that MySQL or MariaDB processes consistently run on the same physical cores, the system can avoid the overhead of migrating processes between cores, which can reduce performance. Additionally, configuring the hypervisor to ensure that the MySQL or MariaDB VM has dedicated access to certain CPU cores, especially in high-traffic environments, can help prevent resource contention and ensure that the database has sufficient processing power for query execution.

Another critical resource to optimize in virtualized environments is memory. Virtualized environments typically rely on shared memory resources, which can lead to memory contention if the host machine is running multiple VMs simultaneously. Inadequate memory allocation for the MySQL or MariaDB VM can lead to increased disk swapping, which significantly degrades performance. MySQL and MariaDB are memory-intensive applications, and optimizing memory usage is vital for ensuring that queries are processed efficiently. The key parameter to tune in this regard is the innodb_buffer_pool_size. The buffer pool is used by InnoDB to cache data and index pages in memory, reducing the need to access data from disk. In virtualized environments, it is crucial to allocate enough memory for the buffer pool to ensure that most data is stored in memory, minimizing disk I/O. As a rule of thumb, the buffer pool should be sized to use about 70-80% of the available memory on the VM, ensuring that enough memory is reserved for the operating system and other processes running on the VM.

However, when tuning memory in a virtualized environment, DBAs should be cautious not to over-allocate memory, as this could impact the performance of other VMs running on the same host. Memory over-allocation in virtualized environments can lead to resource contention, where multiple VMs compete for the same physical memory, resulting in swapping or memory thrashing. To avoid this, DBAs should ensure that memory is allocated according to the system's workload and the needs of MySQL or MariaDB. The memory parameters in MySQL, such as sort_buffer_size, read_buffer_size, and join_buffer_size, should also be adjusted based on the VM's available memory to ensure that queries, particularly complex ones, do not consume excessive memory and cause memory pressure.

Disk I/O performance is another critical factor to consider when tuning MySQL or MariaDB for virtualized environments. Disk I/O performance in virtual machines can be impacted by factors such as storage virtualization overhead and contention with other VMs sharing the same physical disk resources. MySQL and MariaDB are sensitive to disk I/O, especially in write-heavy environments, and inefficient disk usage can lead to slow query performance, replication lag, and overall system instability. In virtualized environments, it is essential to use high-performance storage solutions, such as SSDs, to minimize disk latency. The storage configuration must also be optimized to ensure that MySQL and MariaDB have sufficient throughput for both read and write operations.

For optimal disk I/O performance, configuring the underlying storage layer to use dedicated virtual disk drives (VMDKs) or using DirectStorage (where the virtual machine directly accesses the physical disk) can help minimize the overhead introduced by virtualization. Additionally, tuning the innodb_flush_log_at_trx_commit and innodb_log_file_size parameters can help optimize disk I/O for write-heavy environments. The innodb_flush_log_at_trx_commit parameter controls how frequently InnoDB writes changes to disk, and reducing this value can improve performance by reducing the number of disk flushes, though at the cost of potential data loss during crashes. Increasing the innodb_log_file_size can also help reduce the frequency of log file flushes, improving performance for write-intensive applications.

Networking performance in virtualized environments can be another potential bottleneck, particularly when there is high network traffic between virtual machines or between the virtual machine and external resources. MySQL and MariaDB rely on fast, low-latency network connections for replication, backup, and client-server communication. To optimize networking in virtualized environments, DBAs should ensure that the VM is configured to use high-performance virtual network interfaces, such as the Virtio driver for Linux-based virtual machines, which reduces network overhead. Additionally, it is important to ensure that network traffic between MySQL or MariaDB instances is separated from other traffic on the host to avoid network congestion and ensure reliable performance.

When tuning MySQL or MariaDB in a virtualized environment, it is also essential to monitor resource utilization continually. Virtualized environments often involve dynamic resource allocation, where CPU, memory, and disk resources can be adjusted in real-time. Using monitoring tools, such as the MySQL Enterprise Monitor, Percona Monitoring and Management (PMM), or other third-party solutions, helps track resource usage, identify bottlenecks, and ensure that the database is running efficiently. These tools allow DBAs to observe key performance metrics, such as query execution times, replication lag, and disk I/O throughput, which provide insights into areas that may require optimization.

Optimizing MySQL and MariaDB for virtualized environments requires careful consideration of system resources and the unique challenges introduced by virtualization. By properly allocating CPU, memory, disk, and network resources, and tuning MySQL parameters to suit the virtualized environment, DBAs can ensure that their database systems perform efficiently, even under heavy workloads. Regular monitoring, resource management, and adjustments to system parameters are crucial to maintaining optimal performance in virtualized environments, ensuring that MySQL and MariaDB continue to deliver fast, reliable, and scalable database solutions.

High-Availability Strategies for MySQL and MariaDB

High availability (HA) is a critical requirement for modern database environments, particularly those used in mission-critical applications where downtime can result in significant business disruption. For MySQL and MariaDB, ensuring that the database remains available and resilient to failures involves implementing strategies that minimize downtime, enable automatic failover, and maintain data consistency. Given the increasing reliance on database-driven applications, understanding and implementing effective high-availability strategies for MySQL and MariaDB is essential to ensure that databases perform reliably and remain accessible even in the face of hardware failures, network issues, or other disruptions.

One of the primary methods for achieving high availability in MySQL and MariaDB is through replication. MySQL and MariaDB support a variety of replication models, with master-slave replication being the most commonly used. In this configuration, one server, the master, handles all write operations, while one or more slave servers replicate the data from the master and handle read queries. This setup increases scalability by offloading read traffic from the master server. However, while master-slave replication can enhance performance and provide redundancy, it does not automatically address failover, which is a crucial aspect of high availability. In the event of a master failure, manual intervention is typically required to promote a slave to be the new master, leading to some downtime.

To address this limitation, MySQL and MariaDB offer solutions such as semi-synchronous replication, which ensures that data is written to at least one slave before the transaction is considered committed. This configuration provides better data durability and reduces the risk of data loss in the event of a master failure. Although semi-synchronous replication enhances failover reliability, it still does not fully automate the failover process, making it necessary to implement additional mechanisms to promote a slave to master status automatically. To achieve fully automated failover, tools like Orchestrator or MHA (MySQL High Availability) can be used. These tools monitor the master-slave relationship, automatically detecting when a master fails and promoting a slave to be the new master without requiring manual intervention. This approach reduces downtime and ensures that the database remains available during server failures.

For environments that require even greater availability, MySQL and MariaDB support multi-master replication setups. In a multi-master configuration, multiple nodes are capable of handling both read and write operations, ensuring that no single server becomes a point of failure. This approach is particularly useful in high-traffic applications where both read and write loads are substantial, as it balances the load across several servers and provides fault tolerance. MariaDB, for example, supports Galera Cluster, which implements synchronous multi-master replication, ensuring that all nodes are consistent with each other and can handle both read and write operations. This model guarantees that all transactions are replicated across all nodes in the cluster, which minimizes the risk of data inconsistencies and ensures that the system remains operational even if one node fails.

While multi-master replication provides high availability, it also introduces complexity, particularly with conflict resolution. When multiple nodes can accept writes, there is a potential for data conflicts if two nodes try to modify the same piece of data simultaneously. Galera Cluster handles this issue by using a certification protocol that ensures transactions are conflict-free before they are committed. If a conflict is detected, the transaction is rejected on one of the nodes, preventing data inconsistencies from spreading throughout the cluster. However, multi-master replication systems require careful design to ensure that the replication topology and conflict resolution mechanisms are properly configured, and they may require additional resources to maintain the consistency and performance of the cluster.

Another critical component of high availability is automatic failover. While replication and multi-master configurations help ensure that data is replicated across multiple servers, failover mechanisms are required to automatically promote a replica to the primary server in the event of a failure. Tools such as MySQL Group Replication and MariaDB's built-in Galera Cluster provide built-in failover capabilities. In these systems, when the primary node fails, the cluster automatically selects another node to take over as the master, ensuring that the application experiences minimal downtime. This automatic failover capability is crucial for maintaining high availability in production environments where downtime is unacceptable. Additionally, these systems often include mechanisms for network partitioning and ensuring that only one primary node is accessible, preventing split-brain scenarios where two nodes may both believe they are the master.

Another approach to enhancing the high availability of MySQL and MariaDB is through the use of load balancers. Load balancers can be placed between the application and the database servers to distribute traffic across multiple replicas. By doing so, load balancers reduce the load on any single database server, improve performance, and ensure that traffic is directed to healthy servers. In scenarios where read-heavy workloads are common, load balancers can direct read queries to replicas, while write queries can be directed to the master node or one of the multi-master nodes. This distribution ensures that the database infrastructure can handle higher volumes of traffic without sacrificing performance or availability.

In addition to replication and failover, it is essential to consider the network infrastructure and redundancy in high-availability setups. Network issues can cause delays in replication, result in split-brain scenarios, or disrupt the availability of the database. Ensuring that the network is redundant and highly available is essential to maintaining consistent database performance. Techniques such as using multiple network paths between nodes, implementing network load balancers, and ensuring that network latency is minimal can help improve the resilience of the system. For example, in multi-master setups, it is crucial to have low-latency and high-bandwidth connections between all nodes to minimize the time it takes for transactions to propagate across the cluster.

Backup strategies also play a crucial role in high-availability systems. While replication ensures that the data is available across multiple nodes, it does not protect against data corruption or other types of failures that may occur at the database or application level. Regular, automated backups are necessary to protect data from such issues. Backups should be taken from multiple nodes, including the master and replicas, to ensure that the most current data can be restored in the event of a disaster. Additionally, backups should be stored in geographically separate locations to protect against regional failures. Combining replication with robust backup strategies ensures that the system can recover quickly and efficiently from both minor issues and catastrophic failures.

Monitoring and alerting systems are also critical to high-availability strategies. Constant monitoring of database performance, replication lag, server health, and failover status allows DBAs to detect issues before they become critical. Tools like Percona Monitoring and Management (PMM), MySQL Enterprise Monitor, or custom monitoring scripts can provide real-time insights into the status of the replication process, resource utilization, and overall server health. Configuring appropriate alerts for events such as replication lag, disk space utilization, or node failures can help DBAs respond quickly and take corrective action before issues affect the availability of the system.

High availability in MySQL and MariaDB involves a combination of replication strategies, failover mechanisms, load balancing, network redundancy, backup strategies, and continuous monitoring. By implementing a robust high-availability architecture, organizations can ensure that their databases remain responsive, scalable, and fault-tolerant, even in the face of hardware failures, network issues, or other disruptions. Effective high-availability solutions not only reduce downtime but also improve the overall performance and reliability of MySQL and MariaDB databases, enabling businesses to maintain uninterrupted access to their critical data.

Implementing Read-Write Splitting with MySQL and MariaDB

Read-write splitting is a powerful technique used to optimize database performance by separating read and write operations across different servers. In high-traffic environments, where there is a significant disparity between the number of read and write queries, read-write splitting can dramatically improve scalability, reduce load on the master server, and enhance the overall efficiency of the database system. In MySQL and MariaDB, read-write splitting involves directing write queries to the master server and read queries to one or more replicas, thus balancing the workload and improving response times. Implementing read-write splitting requires careful configuration, monitoring, and load balancing, but when done effectively, it can result in substantial performance gains.

The basic concept behind read-write splitting is to leverage the fact that read queries are typically far more numerous than write queries in most applications. By routing read queries to replica servers, which are synchronized with the master server, the load on the master is reduced, allowing it to handle write operations more efficiently. This setup improves the overall throughput of the database system and ensures that read-heavy workloads do not impact the performance of write operations. MySQL and MariaDB provide built-in support for replication, which is the foundation for read-write splitting. Replicas continuously copy data from the master server, ensuring that they stay up to date and can serve read queries with minimal latency.

Setting up read-write splitting in MySQL or MariaDB begins with configuring replication. In a typical setup, the master server handles all write operations (INSERT, UPDATE, DELETE), while one or more replicas handle read queries (SELECT). The first step is to configure replication between the master and the replicas. In MySQL or MariaDB, this can be achieved using either asynchronous or semi-synchronous replication. In asynchronous replication, the master sends updates to the replicas, but there is no guarantee that the replicas will immediately receive the changes. In semi-synchronous replication, the master waits for at least one replica to acknowledge the receipt of the update before confirming the write operation. For read-write splitting, semi-synchronous replication is often preferred, as it ensures a higher level of consistency between the master and replicas.

Once replication is configured, the next step is to set up the application to route read and write queries to the appropriate servers. This can be done using a load balancer or a proxy layer that is responsible for directing queries based on their type. For example, read queries, which are typically SELECT statements, can be routed to replicas, while write queries, such as INSERT, UPDATE, and DELETE, should be directed to the master server. There are various ways to implement this, depending on the architecture of the system and the available tools.

One popular option is to use a proxy such as ProxySQL, which sits between the application and the MySQL or MariaDB servers, automatically routing read and write queries to the appropriate nodes.

ProxySQL is an advanced proxy layer designed specifically to handle read-write splitting in MySQL and MariaDB environments. It provides features like connection pooling, query routing, and load balancing, making it an excellent choice for managing read-write splitting in large-scale applications. ProxySQL can be configured to identify read queries based on SQL syntax or application-defined rules and automatically route them to replicas, while write queries are sent to the master. It also supports intelligent load balancing, distributing queries across multiple replicas to prevent any single replica from becoming a bottleneck. By leveraging ProxySQL, administrators can implement read-write splitting without requiring significant changes to the application code.

Another approach to read-write splitting is to use built-in features in MySQL and MariaDB such as the read_only system variable. By configuring replicas as read-only, the database automatically restricts write operations on these servers, ensuring that all write queries are directed to the master server. While this approach does not include advanced routing features like ProxySQL, it is a simple and effective way to implement basic read-write splitting in environments where advanced proxying and load balancing are not required.

Load balancing is another critical aspect of implementing read-write splitting. In a setup with multiple replicas, distributing read queries evenly across all replicas can help ensure that no single replica becomes overloaded. Load balancing can be achieved using tools like ProxySQL or HAProxy, which can intelligently distribute queries based on server health, query volume, or custom-defined rules. For example, if one replica is experiencing high load, the load balancer can route queries to other replicas with more available resources, ensuring that the system remains responsive. Additionally, load balancing helps improve fault tolerance, as traffic can be rerouted to healthy servers in the event of a replica failure.

One of the challenges of read-write splitting is ensuring data consistency across the master and replicas. Since the master server handles write operations and the replicas are read-only, there is always a lag between when a write is committed on the master and when the replicas are updated. This replication lag can lead to situations where a client querying a replica might not see the most recent data written to the master. To mitigate this, it is essential to monitor replication lag and adjust the application's behavior accordingly. For example, applications may need to implement a brief delay before routing read queries to replicas after a write operation to ensure that the replica has caught up with the master. This is particularly important in scenarios where real-time consistency is critical, such as in financial or inventory systems.

To handle replication lag more effectively, MySQL and MariaDB offer tools and features that help monitor and manage replication performance. The SHOW SLAVE STATUS command in MySQL and MariaDB provides detailed information about the replication process, including the replication delay (i.e., the Seconds_Behind_Master field). Monitoring this metric is crucial to ensuring that replicas are synchronized with the master and to identifying any issues that could cause excessive lag. Additionally, the pt-heartbeat tool from Percona can be used to measure replication lag in real-time, providing more granular insights into replication performance.

Another strategy to reduce replication lag is to optimize the underlying hardware and network infrastructure. Since replication involves continuous data transfer between the master and replicas, network latency and bandwidth can impact replication speed. Ensuring that the master and replicas are located on the same network, preferably in the same data center or region, can minimize network delays and improve replication performance. Additionally, using high-performance storage solutions, such as SSDs, can reduce disk I/O and improve the speed at which data is written and replicated.

While read-write splitting can provide significant performance benefits, it is important to remember that it is not a one-size-fits-all solution. The effectiveness of read-write splitting depends on the specific workload of the application and the system architecture. For read-heavy applications, read-write splitting can significantly improve scalability and reduce the load on the master server. However, in write-heavy applications, where write operations are frequent and the need for consistency is high, read-write splitting may require more careful configuration to ensure data consistency and prevent replication lag from affecting application performance.

Implementing read-write splitting with MySQL and MariaDB requires a combination of proper replication setup, intelligent query routing, load balancing, and careful monitoring of replication lag. By leveraging tools such as ProxySQL, HAProxy, and built-in MySQL and MariaDB features, organizations can significantly improve the performance and scalability of their database systems. Read-write splitting not only helps balance the load between the master and replicas but also enhances the responsiveness and availability of the database, making it a valuable strategy for high-traffic applications.

Best Practices for Maintenance and Upgrades of MySQL and MariaDB

Maintaining and upgrading MySQL and MariaDB databases is a critical aspect of ensuring the long-term stability, security, and performance of a database-driven application. Proper maintenance practices help ensure the health of the database by addressing issues such as performance degradation, data corruption, and security vulnerabilities. Upgrading to newer versions of MySQL or MariaDB is equally important, as it brings enhancements in features, performance improvements, and bug fixes. However, both maintenance and upgrades must be handled carefully to avoid downtime, data loss, or degradation of service. The best practices for maintenance and upgrades can help mitigate risks and ensure that databases continue to operate efficiently under increasing loads.

One of the first aspects to consider in database maintenance is regular backups. Backing up MySQL and MariaDB databases is essential for data recovery in case of failures, whether due to hardware malfunctions, human error, or software bugs. Backups should be taken regularly, and the frequency of backups should depend on the size of the database and the criticality of the data. It is also recommended to implement a backup strategy that includes full backups, incremental backups, and transaction log backups. Full backups capture the entire database at a specific point in time, while incremental backups only capture the changes made since the last backup. Transaction log backups are crucial for point-in-time recovery, allowing DBAs to restore the database to any specific time. To ensure that backups are reliable, it is important to test them regularly by performing restores in a test environment.

In addition to regular backups, DBAs should implement strategies for monitoring and optimizing the database's performance. Over time, MySQL and MariaDB databases can experience performance degradation due to factors such as inefficient queries, growing datasets, or improper configurations. Regular monitoring of key metrics, such as query execution times, server load, disk I/O, and memory usage, is essential for identifying and addressing performance bottlenecks. Tools like MySQL Enterprise Monitor, Percona Monitoring and Management (PMM), or the performance_schema in MariaDB can provide valuable insights into database performance. Identifying slow queries and optimizing them can lead to significant performance improvements. DBAs should also regularly review database indexes, ensuring that indexes are being used efficiently and removing unnecessary or redundant indexes that can slow down write operations.

Another aspect of regular maintenance is updating and optimizing database configurations. MySQL and MariaDB provide many configuration options that control how the database engine handles memory, disk I/O, and query processing. Over time, the database workload may change, necessitating adjustments to these configurations. Common areas to focus on include the innodb_buffer_pool_size, which controls the amount of memory allocated to the InnoDB storage engine for caching data and indexes, and the max_connections setting, which controls the number of simultaneous connections allowed. Optimizing these settings based on the available system resources can significantly improve database performance. It is also important to keep an eye on database growth and adjust parameters such as table partitioning and disk space allocation to accommodate increasing data sizes.

Database maintenance also includes regular integrity checks. Over time, data corruption can occur due to hardware failures, software bugs, or improper shutdowns. Running integrity checks on MySQL and MariaDB databases is essential to detect and resolve issues before they cause significant problems. The CHECK TABLE command in MySQL and MariaDB can be used to check the integrity of individual tables, while the mysqlcheck utility can be used to check, repair, and optimize all tables in a database. If any issues are detected, such as corrupted indexes or missing data, they should be addressed promptly to avoid more serious consequences. Additionally, routine updates to the underlying operating system and database software should be performed to ensure that any known bugs or vulnerabilities are patched.

Upgrading MySQL and MariaDB is another essential part of database maintenance. Regularly upgrading to newer versions ensures that the database benefits from the latest performance improvements, bug fixes, and security patches. However, upgrading should not be taken lightly, as it can introduce breaking changes or compatibility issues that affect the database application. Before upgrading, DBAs should thoroughly review the release notes for the new version and evaluate whether any changes to database features, configurations, or syntax will impact the application. It is also essential to test the upgrade process in a staging environment to identify any potential issues before applying the changes to the production system.

The first step in upgrading MySQL or MariaDB is to back up the database. Having a reliable backup ensures that, in the event of an issue during the upgrade process, the database can be restored to its previous state. After creating a backup, DBAs should also verify that the system is running optimally and that all hardware resources are functioning as expected. It is also recommended to disable automatic updates on production systems to prevent unexpected changes during the upgrade process.

The actual upgrade process involves several steps, including stopping the database service, applying the upgrade, and performing post-upgrade checks. MySQL and MariaDB provide tools such as mysql_upgrade and mariadb-upgrade that help upgrade the database schema, check for compatibility issues, and optimize the system after the upgrade. These tools ensure that any changes made to the database structure are properly applied, and any deprecated features are handled correctly. It is important to carefully follow the upgrade instructions provided by the MySQL or MariaDB documentation to avoid errors.

After upgrading, DBAs should perform extensive testing to ensure that the application is functioning correctly and that there are no performance regressions. Monitoring the database after an upgrade is essential to ensure that the system is performing as expected and that no new issues have been introduced. Key areas to monitor include query performance, replication status (if applicable), and resource utilization.

For high-availability systems, it is essential to carefully plan the upgrade process to minimize downtime and avoid service interruptions. In a replicated setup, DBAs can perform the upgrade on one replica at a time, promoting each replica to the master role as needed. This approach ensures that the system remains operational during the upgrade process and that there is no single point of failure. When upgrading multi-master setups, it is important to ensure that the new version supports the replication features in use, and that all nodes are upgraded consistently.

As part of ongoing maintenance, DBAs should regularly review and optimize database schema designs. Over time, data models may need to be adjusted to accommodate changes in business requirements or application functionality. Regularly reviewing and updating indexes, table structures, and relationships can help ensure that queries remain efficient as the database grows. For example, as new indexes are added, old, unused indexes should be removed to reduce overhead during write operations.

Effective maintenance and regular upgrades are essential to keeping MySQL and MariaDB databases running efficiently. Proper backup strategies, performance monitoring, and integrity checks ensure that the database remains stable, while timely upgrades ensure that the database benefits from the latest features and improvements. By following best practices for database maintenance and upgrades, DBAs can ensure that their MySQL and MariaDB systems continue to deliver reliable, high-performance results for their applications.

www.ingramcontent.com/pod-product-compliance
Lightning Source LLC
LaVergne TN
LVHW051232050326
832903LV00028B/2364